COLLEGE BOUND

Kathleen Winkler

SAINT LOUIS

Copyright © 1998 Concordia Publishing House
3558 S. Jefferson Avenue, St. Louis, MO 63118-3968
Manufactured in the United States of America

Library of Congress Cataloging-in-Publication Data

Winkler, Kathleen.
    College Bound / Kathleen Winkler.
    p.   cm.
    ISBN 0-570-05313-7
    1. College student orientation—United States—Handbooks, manuals, etc.
I. Title.
LB2343.32.W56   1998
378.1'98—dc21   97-33548

3 4 5 6 7 8 9 10 11   07 06 05 04 03 02 01 00 99

Contents

INTRODUCTION

The dream propelled me from sound asleep to wide awake. My heart pounded, sweat trickled down my neck. It was a few weeks before I was to head off to college. I dreamed I was wandering the campus, trying to find a classroom where I was to take a test. But since I'd never attended the class, I didn't know where to go, and I had no idea what the test was on.

That was 30 years ago, but I remember the dream. Since then I've learned that research shows many students have similar dreams—it's a way for the subconscious to express anxiety.

Are you feeling anxious?

One college admissions advisor conducted a survey of incoming freshman the summer before they started, asking them what they were excited about and what they were most worried about. The answers turned out to be opposite sides of the same coin:

- They were excited about meeting new and different people; they were worried about getting along with them and being lonely.

- They were excited about being more independent; they were worried about handling new responsibilities and making decisions on their own.

- They were excited about having fun; they were worried about alcohol, drugs, and the party atmosphere.
- They were excited about being challenged intellectually; they were worried about doing well.
- They were excited about living away from home; they were worried about being homesick.

If that sounds like you, guess what: You're normal. There'd be something wrong with you if you weren't a bit anxious. Going off to college for the first time is a *major* life change. Think about what's going to be different:

- Your closest friendships.
- The physical space you live in.
- The way you eat—no more of mom's cooking.
- The way you attend classes, study, and even think—all will be very different from high school.
- Your responsibilities—you'll be running your own life from finances to laundry.
- Your spiritual life—college will present a world of both familiar and new temptations. You will either let God slip from your life or grow closer to Him.

That's a lot of change to absorb at one time. But relax. You're not alone. " 'For I know the plans I have for you,' declares the LORD, 'plans to prosper you and not to harm you, plans to give you a hope and a future. Then you will call upon Me and come and pray to Me, and I will listen to you' " (Jeremiah 29:11–12). Those plans include both your salvation and the experiences you will have in college. Face the changes ahead of you with the confidence that Christ is with you every step of the way.

There are two ways to approach leaving for college. You can throw your stuff in a bag, drive to the campus, and hope for the best. Or, you can prepare in advance.

You can learn what life is like on a college campus today by talking to people who have been there and reading books such as this one. You can think through what kind of experience you are looking for, make some mental plans about what you want your college years to be, pray for the Lord's guidance, and then, prepared and ready, go for it.

You might start by thinking about your role in high school and whether you want to continue it in college. Remember, when you leave for college you leave behind the **you** from high school. No one at college knows who you were for the last four years, no one cares. Your reputation and that dumb thing you did that no one would let you forget won't follow you. You have a clean slate and a chance to be the person you want to be.

Were you very shy in high school? Didn't have many friends? Didn't date much? You can change that. You can go out of your way to be friendly, to say hi to people in classes, the dorm, or the cafeteria. You can become a more social person.

Were you one of the ultra-popular people in high school? You need to realize that you'll be a very small fish in a very big pond at college. Do you want to stay in the popular role? You may—then fraternity or sorority life may be right for you. Or, you may find that being popular isn't, by itself, that important anymore. Maybe you want to be more intellectual, maybe you want fewer but more in-depth friendships. You have that choice.

Were you a top student in high school? It will be harder in college but you can still work for all A's. Or, you can decide a balanced life is more important. I hope you won't decide that grades don't matter at all and spend all your time partying—but that's also a choice you can make.

Were you an athlete in high school? You already know the competition will be tougher in college. Do you want to stay with the same sport? Try something new? Do you want to continue in sports at all? It's your choice.

You can be who you choose to be in college. *Choose wisely.*

Today's college campus is going to be very different from your high school. The college will consider you an adult: That means you will be in charge of your life and your choices. No one will tell you when or how much to study or when to come in. No one will tell you what to eat, how much to sleep, or when to wash clothes so you won't run out of clean socks. Colleges say they give students a lot of guidance on choosing courses and majors but the truth is, it will probably be mostly up to you. You'll have a chance to spread your wings and fly on your own, for better or for worse.

There's tremendous value in a college education. First and foremost, there's the satisfaction of being an educated person, someone who is prepared to deal with the complexities of modern society. Economically there's a big advantage attached to that college degree too: People with a college education earn many thousands of dollars more over a lifetime than do nongraduates. Many interesting occupations, especially in technical fields, are closed to you without that magic piece of paper.

But there are also some other benefits from the years you'll spend in college. You'll make life-long friendships. You probably have some very close friends from high school, and many of those relationships will last through the years. But your college friendships will be even more intense—you will, after all, live with these people in a way you didn't with high school friends. Many adults are still close to people they were friends with in college—even after 30 years I can call Melba or Karen and just pick up where we left off. And remember, at college you very well may meet the person with whom you will spend the rest of your life—I didn't, but both my kids did.

Then there are the fun and the memories that will last a lifetime. I can still picture the dorm rooms I lived in, smell the campus in spring when the flowers were in bloom, hear the clink of glasses and the murmur of conversation in the dining hall, and hear the swell of the organ in chapel as if it were yesterday. I remember trick-or-treating on Halloween night, the toothpaste Barb put in the Oreo cookies, the time we pasted newspapers across Sue's doorframe so when she opened the door she was greeted by a sea of black and white. Your memories won't be the same as mine or your parents' or your brother's or your best friend's. They will be unique to you. But you will have them, and you will carry them with you for the rest of your life.

As a Christian college student you have a special opportunity as well as a special responsibility. You'll have a chance to grow in your faith and to share it with others whether you are on a Christian or a secular campus. Opportunities for worship and Bible study exist on every campus, religious or not. The chance to quietly witness about your faith will present itself over and over again—in class, in late night dorm discussions, in one-on-one conversations with friends and dates.

Your parents, and God working through them, are offering you a very special opportunity in giving you a chance to go to college. It's an opportunity not everyone has. Take advantage of it.

Decide what you want to get out of the next four (or more) years. Talk to your parents about it. Talk to God about it. Go into it as ready as anyone can be.

Remember that no matter where you are going to school, God will be there. He cares about you as His special child—enough to give His Son for you. He wants you to have the best possible experience at college. He wants it to be a time to grow in His grace and love. When you pack your things for the big move, don't leave Him behind. Welcome God into your college life and He will bless it.

Then, with God and your parents firmly supporting you, plunge deeply into your new world. Grab hold of every opportunity to learn and grow. Study hard, play hard, open yourself to others, form bonds, savor every minute of your college experience. It will never come again in quite the same way, and you'll never regret putting your all into it to gain the most you can.

Good luck and God bless!

Kathy Winkler

1

Mom and Dad Just Drove Away— What Do I Do Now?

Adjusting to Life on Campus

"Hooray, I'm free at last—on my own!"

"I miss Mom and Dad—and my dog—so much. I never thought I'd say this, but I even miss my little brother."

"I had such close friends in high school. Here I'm all alone. What am I going to do without them?"

New students' reactions to being transported out of the cozy cocoon of family and high school and dropped into the middle of the alien universe of college run the gamut from ecstasy to terror. About the only thing that applies across the board: Whatever you're feeling as that license plate fades in the distance is normal. After all, you are facing a major life change. Wouldn't it be a little odd if you weren't nervous about

- missing family and friends?
- making new friends, especially if you don't know anyone at your college?

- living in a room the size of a shoebox with someone you've never met and whose habits you know nothing about?
- getting comfortable with a new campus, new city, perhaps a whole new area of the country?
- eating cafeteria food 21 meals a week—and missing Mom's cooking?
- managing your time, finances, and checkbook?
- doing your laundry without turning all your underwear pink?

That's a lot to worry about. It's no wonder many new college students spend the first weeks, even months, in a fog of uncertainty, homesickness, and confusion. Slowness to adjust to college living is one of the major reasons kids pack up and head home. Rachel, who spent her junior year as an RA (Resident Assistant—get used to the term, they will become very important people in your life) in a dorm full of freshmen, remembers one girl who only stayed three days before she cashed it in and went home. "That's not nearly enough time," Rachel says. "You have to remember that homesickness will go away. It *will* get better."

One way to avoid spending those first few weeks in misery is to be prepared—to know what things about campus life trip up new students so you are as ready as possible to handle them.

"I see four things that cause kids trouble when they first come to college," says Patricia Prischman, director of residence life at the University of Wisconsin, Milwaukee, a large urban university which includes three high-rise dorm towers that are home to more than 2,000 students. Let's take a look at what she sees as issues for new students.

1. **New students have a need for affiliation.** In plain language, that means that you need to know you fit in, to make friends, to become a part of your college rather than just an onlooker. Prischman says that students often don't feel they are a part of their school for the whole first year. "After that they begin to feel they are college people," she says. "But at first, they often feel like a homeless person who just happens to be at college!"

2. **New students often don't live in "day-tight compartments."** That term, coined by Andrew Carnegie, means living one day at a time, living in today, not spending energy on tomorrow or yesterday. A new college student who gets a D on a chemistry quiz, for example, may immediately flip through a mental catalog of disasters that will happen next—I'm going to fail this course, I'll lose my scholarship, I'll have to drop out and go to work. "And all over a chemistry quiz," Prischman laughs. "New students often don't see things for what they are; everything takes on way more weight than it should."

   Even though my own transition to college life happened 30 years ago, I remember a devotion led by a wise RA one of the first nights. The message was *one day at a time*. She urged her flock of shell-shocked freshman not to think in terms of four years of tests, papers, and dorm life but to think only about getting through today. That was good advice then, it still is now.

3. **New students feel the pull of noncollege friends.** New students have one foot in college and one in their old town, Prischman says. Friends who haven't chosen college and instead have gone to work probably have a lot more money, maybe a new

car, more time for social life, less stress. It can look pretty attractive from behind a pile of books. You have to keep in mind the value of long-term goals versus short-term gratification. That can be hard through a fog of discouragement and homesickness.

4. **New students fail to "seek recovery."** There are lots of wrong roads new students can turn down: Hanging out with the party-don't-study crowd, giving in to financial pressures and working too much so you can have more spending money, depending on alcohol to keep stress under control, ignoring low grades rather than dealing with academic problems. Solutions? There are so many, says Prischman. "Learn what's important in friends and pick better ones. Find a mentor who can stop what I call 'stinking thinking' and give you better ways to cope. Talk to the prof in a course that's giving you trouble." She also points out that colleges provide all sorts of avenues to help: RAs, residence directors, campus social services, and counseling centers. Too many students don't use them until it's too late.

In the interest of making the transition from "homeless person roaming campus" to college student easier, let's take a closer look at several practical issues of college life.

Planning Ahead

Just the idea of packing up your wardrobe and the contents of your room and moving them to a new location can be overwhelming. It's easier if you have some guidelines on what to bring and what to leave behind. Here are some tips gathered from various college students:

1. Plan your clothing needs carefully.

Remember, you'll only have half of a closet the size of your mom's broom closet and a couple of dresser drawers. If you are really lucky, you might get a whole dresser to yourself, but don't count on it. I remember moving my daughter into the dorm and watching in awe as a girl down the hall and her mother hauled in load after load of elegant clothes. The mom looked at the closet and loudly announced, "This is simply unacceptable!" Well, it's reality—you don't have a choice.

Concentrate on the stuff you'll need every day: jeans, T-shirts, sweaters, sweats. You won't need a lot of dress clothes at most colleges although there are exceptions. Remember the weather—you may think you outgrew raincoats and mittens in kindergarten but in college you often have long hikes across campus to your next class in the cold and wet. Pack what you feel most comfortable in—not what your favorite fashion magazine says is "in." Keep in mind that unless your college has private bathrooms you may have to head down the hall to a community bathroom and there could be persons of the opposite sex roaming the hall, so bring something for modesty. Avoid stuff that needs to be dry cleaned or ironed—you won't do it. You'll run out of socks and underwear first, so bring a lot. Shoes take up room, so limit them to ones that go with the most clothes. Leave expensive, "real" jewelry at home—why tempt anyone?

2. Pick appropriate stuff for your room.

Dorm rooms are amazing—the day you move in they are as bare and cold as a monk's cell. After a few weeks all the rooms are transformed—warm and cozy—they look like people's homes. It takes a lot to accomplish that transformation but be realistic. There's only so much room!

Coordinate things with your roommate ahead of time to avoid duplication. You don't both need a refrigerator (most schools rent them—check before buying), telephone, stereo, TV, and microwave. You certainly won't have room for two couches. You might not even need two hairdryers if you don't mind sharing. A lot of students build lofts in their room for sleeping, leaving the entire floor area free for living. Lofts are great space-savers if your school permits them (in most schools they have to be free-standing so you don't put bolts in the wall). You can split the cost of lumber with your roommate and build it yourself or buy one from a student who is leaving.

Your bed will be the center of your life, so make it comfortable. A washable spread or quilt you can just yank up is best. A stuffed backrest can make the bed a great place to read or study—unless you fall asleep! Find out in advance the mattress size—at some schools they are extra-long and require special sheets.

You'll need bookshelves—you won't believe how fast your collection of text and reference books will grow. Most dorms provide a desk, but you may need a separate stand if you are taking a computer (find out if there's a lab and how hard it is to get computer time before deciding to bring your own). A file cabinet can help keep you organized. A coat rack is a handy place to fling jackets, bathrobes, and towels. A basket or trunk can hold a lot of stuff and double as a coffee table.

Posters, pictures, flags, bulletin or message boards, throw rugs, carpet remnants, pillows, bamboo shades, strings of beads as room dividers, Christmas lights all year round, plants—the things students use to decorate their spaces—are limited only by imagination. Here's the place to go wild and make it your own. Again, coordinate these plans with your roommate.

A word about your door—make it tell who you are. Name plaques are great and an erasable message board is handy. One friend in Brad's dorm decorated his door with newspaper cartoons; the collection gradually crept down the hall. There were always a few guys hanging around reading.

If you and your roommate have different decorating tastes (like Lynn who loves earth tones and got a roommate who wanted pink and blue ruffles on everything), you'll have to work out a compromise. Half the room in each style might make a decorator shudder, but it could express each of your personalities.

3. **Bring only necessary sports equipment.**

A lot of students find a bike a real necessity on campus. Make sure it has a strong lock and there is a place to store it in bad weather. If you are into tennis, in-line skating, or other sports, you might want to bring your gear; slamming a tennis ball around can be a great stress reliever and you may meet people who share your interest. A sleeping bag can be handy if you spend the night in someone else's room or at another school.

Roommates: They Make Life Interesting

There's probably nothing else that causes more stress to new college students than getting along with a roommate. A University of Florida at Gainesville survey a few years ago showed that 96 percent of incoming freshmen came from single occupancy bedrooms—in other words, they'd never shared a room before. "When they move into the dorm it quickly becomes, 'I don't like your habits, you don't give me my phone messages, and you're invading my life,'" says Prischman. "Having to compromise, realizing that this person doesn't have to put up with your quirks, that you have to work something out, can be a shock. The biggest things we have to work on with new college students are the very same things we teach in the daycare center—keep the bathroom clean, share, and don't crab about your buddy!" she laughs.

Part of the roommate issue is lack of privacy. "At home you can escape into your own room and get away from everything," says Rachel, the RA. "At school it's your roommate's room also, and you don't have a private place—there's no place to get away."

In the interest of preventing roommate wars, let's look a little more closely at the issues that cause the most trouble.

- **Sharing stuff.** Too many kids the day they move in blithely say, "You can use anything of mine you want." They really don't know how they're going to feel when their roommate wears everything in their closet or doesn't treat their property with respect. (I remember a friend when I was in college who almost killed her roommate for taking a nap in her prized black cashmere sweater.) Be careful what you promise. Perhaps start slowly and, if it works out, share more. On the other hand, be reasonable about your roommate using things that really become "the room's." Rachel remembers one girl who took the phone with her when she left the room and told her roommate she couldn't watch the TV she'd brought unless she was there. Now that's unreasonable. Talk about it before the issue arises and set some ground rules.

- **Cleanliness.** This is a big problem. Some people like things absolutely perfect with nothing an inch out of line—they probably would be happiest in a single room. Others are complete slobs who let mold grow on dirty dishes and never wash their sheets—John used to spray room deodorant into his roommate's bed every couple of days! Those people should probably live alone also. However, in reality there aren't a lot of single rooms and besides, the vast majority of people fall somewhere in the middle of the neatness scale. So, again, talk about it beforehand and set some ground rules: How often you will clean, who will do what, and what degree of neatness is required. Keep in mind, dorm rooms are very small—even a little clutter can make the room look like a landfill.

- **Time schedules.** Just as night people and morning people always seem to marry each other, roommates often have opposite biological clocks. Lynn was an owl who did her best studying at night and often didn't go to bed until 2:00 A.M. Her roommate got up at 5:00 A.M. to blow-dry her long hair (in the room). That was grounds for war. Some colleges try to match morning and night people as roommates but sometimes realities of life conflict—even a night owl may need to get to bed early if he or she gets stuck with a 7:00 A.M. class. Again, you've got to talk about it and set up a reasonable schedule. You might agree that if you want to stay up studying after 11:00 P.M. you'll go to the lounge, or that if you have to get up at the crack of dawn you'll tiptoe around and dry your hair in the bathroom. One semester when I was in college all three of us had an early class at the same time and only one bathroom. We rotated who got up first, second, and third on a daily basis. The last thing before we said goodnight was a check on who was getting up first in the morning.

- **Room visitors.** This can be the hardest of all, especially if the visitor is of the opposite sex. If a roommate's boyfriend or girlfriend is planted in your room all the time, you may feel like you have no home. And if your roommate is having sex in your room, you could be treated to more X-rated scenes than in a movie theater. In these cases you just have to speak up. It is your room too, after all, and you are paying dearly for it. You have a right to use it without constant hassle. If you and your roommate can't work out the issue, you may have to call on your RA. The school will probably be on your side; they don't want nonroommates "camping" in the room any more than you do.

As for the issue of sex, you can try to get your roommate to see the moral aspect, but if he or she doesn't share your faith, that may not be possible. You may have to remember the principle "Hate the sin but love the sinner." Jon, whose roommate was having sex with his girlfriend in their room, finally told him, "Look, you're the one who should be embarrassed about what you're doing, but I end up embarrassed when I walk in on you. Would you at least put a sign on the door!" That might not be the solution for everyone, but it worked for him.

- **Being social friends with your roommate.** It's tempting to hang out socially with your roommate the first days of school because you don't know anybody else. Often, as new friendships develop, you and your roommate may find yourself in different social circles. That's okay, especially if you continue to live together harmoniously. It's also okay to become best friends with your roommate. Just don't put pressure on each other—let it develop as it will. Problems crop up when one person wants to cling while the other moves into new relationships. In that case you have to talk with your roommate and agree how much togetherness you are comfortable with.

By the way, Rachel doesn't recommend rooming with a high school friend because it can be too isolating. "Ask to live on the same floor but don't room together," she advises. "You'll meet your roommate, and her roommate, and the people those two roommates know, and you'll have an instant chain of friends."

Here are some ways to tip the odds of having a positive roommate experience in your favor:

- If your college has a questionnaire to match roommates, be *completely honest* on it. Don't say you are an extrovert if you really tend to shy away from new people and situations. You could end up in a room with a bunch of outgoers socializing and dancing up a storm while you'd kill for some peace and quiet. One college, instead of the usual "smoke-or-not-smoke, stay-up-or-bed-early" questions uses scenarios: Your roommate borrows your sweater without asking and spills beer on it. How upset would you be? They claim they've cut room change requests in half. Your honesty on the questionnaire can help prevent the problems listed above, but remember that you'll still have to compromise on some issues with your roommate.

- If there's a choice of types of dorms, pick one that suits your needs. Many schools offer "cultural awareness" dorms where you can get to know people of other cultures, "wellness" dorms where alcohol and smoking are prohibited (they sometimes include fitness centers), "intensive study" dorms, "single sex" dorms, "coed" dorms, and a bunch of others. If you are thinking of a coed dorm, find out what that means on your campus. Sometimes it means the guys' and girls' wings have a common lobby. Sometimes it means alternate floors, sometimes it means alternate suites in which suitemates of the same sex share a bathroom. Know what you're getting into.

- Try to meet your roommate beforehand or, if that's not possible, at least talk on the phone. If you have some idea of what to expect, some feel for this person's interests and personality, the adjustment will be easier.

- Try not to count first impressions too heavily. You're meeting this person at a very stressful time: Both of your families may be there, you both may be coping with the strain of saying goodbye. Give your new roommate a chance, and then another, and still another if necessary.

- Sit down with your roommate as soon as the confusion dies down and talk about the things we've discussed: Sharing things, morning and night issues, how clean the room is to be kept, even the type of music and TV programs you like best and who gets to choose. Dawn Walker, residence life director at Concordia University, Wisconsin, has drawn up a contract she calls *Roommate Keys* that both parties fill out separately and then exchange. Its questions include

  1. When do you plan to study?
  2. When do you like to sleep?
  3. What kind of music do you listen to? When can it be played?

4. What are your favorite TV programs? When can the TV be on?

5. How would you like to arrange your room?

6. How do you want to keep the room? (very neat, a little mess is okay, I don't care)

7. Is it okay for your roommate to wear your clothes and use your personal items? Under what conditions?

8. Is it okay for your roommate to entertain friends in the room? Opposite sex friends? Under what conditions?

9. Are there other things important to you?

Talking over such a contract can make things go much more smoothly.

When Your Roommate Is Not Like You

Some people walk into their dorm room and find out their roommate is from another country, is of a different race, or has a disability. That can be a shock if you didn't know in advance and, for many students, it can really complicate their adjustment. In this situation the advice to not let first impressions count too strongly goes double, even triple. If your first response is "I've never known a white person, a black person, or someone in a wheelchair, and now I'm supposed to live with one!" that isn't going to make getting to know the person any easier.

You need to first remind yourself of a few lessons God has taught us: He loves and sent His Son to die for everyone in this world, no matter what race or disability, and He holds all of us equal in His love. If we live in response to God's love, then we are required to respect every person. Period.

If you think you can't relate to your roommate because he or she is different, sit down and reflect on where those feelings come from. Did you grow up in a family that was prejudiced? Was there a lot of anti-any-body-different feeling in your high school? Did you ever have a bad experience with a person of another race? If any of those things are true, recognize that your own feelings have been flavored by those experiences and that those feelings can run very deep. However, that doesn't excuse disliking people because of their race or disability; you have the power to control those feelings. The first step is to admit the feelings exist and that you want to change them. Some tips to help:

- **Give the roommate a chance.** Get to know him or her as a real person, not as a "white" or a "black" or a "wheelchair" person. You might simply tell him or her right away, "I've never known a white person, or a black person, or someone with cerebral palsy before, so I'm a little nervous." You may find out he or she feels the same way.

- **Look on it as a learning experience.** "There's so much richness of culture and things to learn in living with a person of another race," says Patricia Prischman. "And what about that person learning about your culture? Leaving will deprive both of you of that."

- **Practice for "real life."** Remember that once you enter the workplace, you will have to deal with people of many cultures and disabilities. This is good training for real life.

- **Deal with conflicts honestly.** If conflicts develop, ask yourself honestly if it's due to race or if that's a coverup for a personality or lifestyle issue that could be worked out.

- **Stick it out.** Bear in mind that being uncomfortable with someone different isn't grounds for changing rooms at most colleges. "The other person doesn't have to move just because you don't like their race or disability—they have rights too," says Dawn Walker.

Walker admits that she herself grew up in a city with racial tension and her perception of black people in particular wasn't very good when she started college. "Then I got to know a lot of people from other races and that opened my eyes to the fact that they are individuals just like me, they have very high intelligence and are capable of being professional in every field," she says. "You'll be a more well-rounded person than if you were never exposed to people different from yourself."

Kristin learned that lesson when she was assigned a roommate from Singapore. "It does give you a chance to learn about another culture," she says, "and to look at your own culture through another person's eyes as you answer 'Why are you doing that?' At the same time, it can be hard to blend two sets of customs; sometimes you or the other person might do something not realizing it's rude in the other culture." Her roommate ate a type of dried fish that filled the room with a strong smell and she recalls a friend's international roommate who cooked a soup of such strong odor that it permeated the whole floor. She suggests a lot of open communication as the remedy for solving these kinds of clashes, as well as give-and-take on both sides. There is one big advantage to having an international roommate she points out—sometimes you get to try a lot of great new foods!

A word about having a homosexual roommate. That situation can hold a special tension for a Christian student. First, recognize that on a secular campus sexual orientation cannot be grounds for a room change. If you object to a gay roommate, Rachel says, the school will see you as being at fault and tell you that you need to become more open-minded. Prischman backs that up. "Just because someone is gay doesn't mean they are going to rape you, or whatever else people fear," she says. "If any person, no matter their sexual orientation, stares at you or makes inappropriate comments about your body, you have to say something. But if you are just afraid of gays because of what others have told you about them, you need to find out more about them as people. We'd change your room if the person actually did something inappropriate, but not just because you don't like it."

In this situation you may feel that you need to witness your Christian faith but you will have to do so very carefully, keeping in mind Peter's instruction to the early Christians: "Always be prepared to give an answer to everyone who asks you to give the reason for the hope that you have. But do this with gentleness and respect, keeping a clear conscience, so that those who speak maliciously against your good behavior in Christ may be ashamed of their slander" (1 Peter 3:15). As Peter reminds us, we put our trust in Jesus for strength to lead a God-pleasing life. And when testifying to our faith, we are to speak in love, not in degrading terms. Rachel points out that many times gay students are among the most unhappy on campus because they feel isolated and that they don't fit in. Reaching out to another human being who is having a tough time can be rewarding.

If Things Really Don't Work

If you and your roommate have had some honest heart-to-hearts and you can't come up with any acceptable compromises, you still have some options to explore.

The first, says Rachel, is a roommate mediation by an RA. She usually has one of the warring parties sleep in her room overnight to give everyone a chance to cool off before tackling the issues. "You can't talk to someone when you're really mad," she says. "If you are so steamed about what set you off, you can't get down to the root of the problem."

Then she sits down with both parties and tries to work out the issues. She allows only "I-feel" statements (when you do this I feel …) no "you" statements (you always do this …). Sometimes that's successful. If not, she says, you work your way up the food chain: The dorm director, the residence life director, maybe the campus counselor. A lot of kids call their parents but Rachel feels that doesn't accomplish anything except having mad parents yelling at the school. "You can't expect your parents to take care of everything," she says. "At some point you have to realize they can't solve your problems for you."

If nothing works, you and the other person may have no choice but to split up. If there's extra room in the dorm, it may just mean packing your stuff and moving. However, if the dorm is full, you may have to stick it out until a spot opens up. More than one set of roommates has strung a line down the middle of the room and led separate lives until a slot became available.

Getting Over the "Homesick Virus"

Suppose you've done all the advance planning you can, you're getting along with your roommate, and your first loads of laundry turned out fine, but you're still homesick. Homesickness isn't funny to the person experiencing it—it can keep you in a cloud of depression and sap your energy so you don't make the effort to change it. Rachel has some suggestions:

- First, and most important, she says: *Get involved.* Most campuses hold some sort of fair in the first few days to let new students know what activities are offered. At her school it's called the "Org Smorg" (Organization Smorgasbord). Go. Since most campuses have a group for every interest and social issue, there's bound to be something that appeals to you. The friends you make in drama, music, or intramural sports can be the ones that last a lifetime. The campus Christian ministry can be a source of friends with the same values you have, and a campus pastor can be a good source of advice and support when things are tough.

- *Go to the social mixers the first few days.* Picnics, dances, movie nights, floor discussions—they're all a chance to meet people. Sitting in your room wallowing in misery won't help you get over it—as corny as a brat fry on the athletic field might sound, it will lift your spirits.

- *Don't go home too often.* If you go home every weekend, Rachel says, you will see your family but you'll still have to say goodbye after two days and you will have missed a lot. "Weekends are when people gather, when they do their socializing and bonding," she says. "People will always invite you along because everybody's in the same boat, not knowing anyone, freshman year."

- *Keep your door open.* People going by will stop to say hello. You have to make an effort too—say hello to people you meet in class, in the halls, in the cafeteria. If you see an open door in the dorm, stop in. The person inside may be as lonely and homesick as you are.

- *Be confident that the feelings will go away.* Just give them time—more than a few days. "When you are at home, you have your family," Rachel says. "It's not exactly that you are transferring your loyalties, but when you are at school, you also have your family—friends and the people you live with."

- *Keep in touch with those at home.* It's easy by phone and especially by e-mail. Rachel is enthused about the possibilities of e-mail. "You can talk to your friends at home or at their colleges 10 times a day if you want to, and it doesn't cost any more than a local phone call," she says.

Campus life is one of the greatest experiences you can have. I still keep in touch with people I lived with in college; a few of them are my closest friends even though 30 years have gone by and we live miles apart. It's all in what you make of it.

"Come in with an open mind," says Dawn Walker. "Living in a residence hall is a huge part of what you will learn in college. It's an important part of growing up and becoming independent—learning to relate and get along with others. There is so much positive about it and so much growth can come from it."

A Word about Fraternities and Sororities

Dorms and apartments aren't the only places to live on many campuses; floor parties and college-sponsored activities are not the only places to meet people. On many campuses the Greek system—fraternities and sororities—offers a chance for increased social life, a way to meet people, even a place to live. Sometimes fraternities and sororities also offer pressure to drink, restriction of the type of people you will meet, and pressure to conform.

Should you join a fraternity or sorority? There's no one answer to that question. It depends on a lot of things:

- Your individual personality and interests.
- The types of Greek organizations on your campus.
- How important the frat/sorority scene is at your school.

Kyle joined a fraternity during his sophomore year and lived in the frat house his last two years of college. He's glad he did.

"I didn't join right away," he says. "I went in with an open mind, looked around to find the right fraternity for me, checked a lot of them out."

He says the fraternities on his campus had different styles and reputations. Some were heavily into the party and drinking scene, one was known for drug use, one was the "snob group" who weren't interested in anyone who wasn't just like them, one was for jocks. Kyle asked questions of fraternity members and of sorority members who often have a good understanding of the different fraternities. "Then I headed for a group that seemed diverse and open, one where I fit in," he says.

His motivation for joining was simple. "I was looking for a family away from home, and that's what I found," he says. "I made very close friends—we still keep in contact even after graduation."

He'd definitely do it again, probably sooner. He has some advice: "Find the one that's right for you," he says. "In my fraternity we had a lot of different types of people; without it we probably wouldn't have met each other."

Rhonda, on the other hand, probably wouldn't join a sorority again if she had it to do over. "My brother and sister had done it and both had a good time, so I just figured it's what everyone does," she says.

She joined right away in her freshman year and moved into the house her sophomore year. At first she really liked it. She met a lot of people, made good friends, had the chance to go to a lot of social activities.

Later, she began to get bored with the whole scene. "You do so many activities that are supposed to promote bonding, but a lot of them are really dumb," she says. "It definitely was a distraction from school. Having to go to a chapter meeting that took a whole evening every Monday got old. Some of the rituals—the robes, the ceremonies—were kind of cultish, sort of creepy."

She felt that joining the sorority held her back from making friends outside the system. "Generally, you only meet people from a higher economic level," she says. "Many of them are so focused on Greek life they don't have anything to do with anyone outside it. It even continues after they graduate—they're almost scared of anybody outside the system. There's a real attitude of conformity."

She also found some racial prejudice—only one minority young woman rushed her sorority and she dropped out before the end. In previous years some minority women had been excluded because of race. That troubled her.

Rhonda also observed a lot of cheating by fraternity and sorority members. Some houses, she said, maintained files on various classes and gave out copies of tests.

And there was a lot of emphasis on drinking. "Every event revolved around alcohol," she says.

"In general, there were more things about it I disliked than I liked," she says. "It wasn't all bad; I would have left if it were. But I probably wouldn't do it again."

If you are considering whether to pledge a fraternity or sorority, consider these pros and cons:

Pros

- You will meet a lot of people and make instant friends. Many of them will become lifelong friends. The closeness and acceptance can stave off pangs of homesickness.
- You may have a nicer place to live. Fraternity and sorority houses can be much more appealing than dorm rooms.
- You'll have instant access to a wide variety of social events and activities.
- If you are having trouble with a course, you can often find a person in your group to tutor you.
- Some fraternities and sororities are into social service; you may find ways to serve others.

Cons

- It costs a lot of money. Figure on at least several hundred dollars a year.
- Joining may restrict the number and kind of people you meet, especially if your group exerts a lot of pressure to do things only with them. There are interesting people out there who aren't in the Greek system.
- There may be pressure to drink, use drugs, or be sexually active.
- It can take a lot of time away from studies.
- Many times people are judged very quickly and on

superficial terms. You may not be offered a bid; rejection can be hard to take.

"Take your time, wait, explore all your options," Rhonda says. "If you do go in, don't be afraid to back out. Don't do anything you're uncomfortable with. Some groups do hazing even though they're not supposed to; you don't have to put up with that. And don't make it the center of your life and cut yourself off from everyone who is non-Greek; that's very limiting."

If you decide to pledge, enjoy it. Make the most of the friendships and the social opportunities. But always be yourself and do what's right for you as a child of God.

2

STAYING HEALTHY— PHYSICALLY AND EMOTIONALLY

"The food was so good at college, but it was really fatty," says Beth. "I think everyone gained the 'Freshman 15.' My weight crept up slowly, but finally I got to 160. I'm about 5' 7" and in high school I weighed 130, so that was too much."

Beth's story isn't unusual. College is a place where your health—both physical and emotional—can plunge downhill fast. Weight gain, obsessive weight loss, mononucleosis, stress, and depression can all be part of college life. But the good news is that your health is largely within your control. Many of the major factors in keeping you healthy physically and emotionally are related to the choices you make.

In this chapter we'll look at a lot of those choices and explore how to keep healthy in many ways: controlling your weight without going overboard, handling stress, avoiding infectious illnesses, coping with depression.

Eating Healthily

No, the major food groups aren't pizza, chocolate, ice cream, and french fries! You know all the rules about healthy eating—you've heard them since grade school, but on campus where opportunities for Big Macs abound and you can't control the cafeteria, it can be hard to eat healthy foods. That, combined with a possible decrease in physical activity, can pad your thighs (women), or your abdomen (men) with a layer of fat pretty quickly.

According to registered dietician Shirley Reiter, a nutrition educator at the Medical College of Wisconsin, there are several factors that cause the common college weight blow-up.

"Most college students don't eat a very good diet," she says. "Remember, you are making your own choices now—Mom's not putting the food on the table anymore." She points out that poor food choices plus the endless snacking that's part of dorm life are the usual culprits.

She offers some dont's and do's for healthier college eating.

Try to avoid the following:

- **Skipping meals, especially breakfast.** Studies show that students who eat breakfast perform better in school. Eating a balanced breakfast helps distribute your calories throughout the day instead of packing them into the afternoon and evening. But be aware that a breakfast of bacon and eggs, hash browns, and buttered toast can total 1,200 calories, half of them from fat. Use breakfast to pick up some grains and fruit.

- **Nightly trips for a 10:00 pizza or hamburger.** "It's fine once in a while, but in moderation," Reiter says.

- **Snacking on junk food while studying.** Ever hear, "I have to keep up my energy while I study"? How many of your dorm-mates have a bowl of M & M's on their desk? Chips and cheese curls are loaded with fat, salt, and sugar but empty of nutrition. If you need to snack while studying, keep fruit, peeled baby carrots, or air-popped popcorn on hand.

- **Bad choices in the cafeteria line, such as fats in gravy or salad dressing.** The salad bar can be a healthy choice if you control the type and amount of dressing and the nuts and bacon bits. It's entirely possible to build a salad that has more calories than the main entree!

- **Dessert with every meal.** No one is saying that you can't ever eat dessert again, but limit rich desserts to once or twice a week. The rest of the time have fruit or a low-calorie treat.

- **Alcohol calories.** Yes, they do count. Although they can't be stored as fat, the body burns them instead of food calories so dinner can go right to your middle.

Instead do the following:

- **Build your diet around the food pyramid.** (See Appendix, page 160.) Note that cereals and grains form the base of the pyramid. They should be the base of your diet. The next biggest category should be fruits and vegetables. Then add in dairy products and meats, and finally eat sparingly from the top—fats and sugars. Too many people, says Reiter, "eat from the top down instead of the bottom up." If your campus offers lots of fast food, try to avoid it. Go to delis or sandwich shops instead. You still get fast, good food, and you avoid a lot of the fat.

Choose food wisely, though. A meatball sub with cheese probably isn't much better for you than a hamburger and fries.

- **Choose whole, not refined, grains—wheat bread instead of white.** Whole grains provide much-needed fiber and minerals. Try keeping granola bars or whole grain breakfast bars or crackers in your room to snack on. Get accustomed to reading nutrition information on food labels. Many low-fat, high-fiber foods add lots of extra sugar to make up for bland taste.

- **Get enough calcium.** The osteoporosis that turns older women's bones to Swiss cheese has its roots in the teens and 20s when the bone base should be built. Choose low-fat dairy products. Reiter notes that 2 percent milk is little better than whole, you need 1 percent or skim. If you have to drink diet soda instead of milk, take a calcium supplement; you won't get the other nutrients available in milk, but at least your bones won't suffer.

- **Include a minimum of five servings of fruits and vegetables.** Reiter points out that fruits today, especially apples, are often huge—a large one can count as two servings. Keep apples, oranges, bananas, or your favorite fruit in your room. Eat fruit between classes or at night while you're studying.

- **Consider a vitamin supplement.** "It can be good insurance," says Reiter, "but remember, it can't replace food." Take vitamins at the recommended level; mega-doses can be dangerous. The more involved you get on campus, the busier you'll be. The busier you get, the more sporadic your meals can become. Keeping staples such as fruit, whole grain bread, sliced turkey, etc., in your dorm room refrigerator can help ensure that you get the nutrients you need. Plan ahead. If you know you're heading off to a busy day and may not get to the dining hall, throw a sandwich or fruit (or both) in your backpack and eat between classes. Don't skip your meals and decide you'll "catch up" by eating a pizza while you study at 10:00 P.M. You'll only get your metabolism out of whack.

- **Construct a vegetarian diet carefully.** Vegetarian eating is becoming very popular on college campuses; Reiter says it's perfectly possible to stay healthy, especially if you eat eggs and dairy products, but it takes careful planning. Get information from your campus health service or the library to be sure you're eating right. "The people most at risk of poor nutrition are vegans who eat no animal products," she says. "They probably should take a B-12 and iron supplement."

If you need to lose weight, remember that a pound is 3,600 calories. Active women can probably handle 2,000–2,200 calories a day; active men can often go up to 2,800. If you are sedentary, you need far fewer calories. There are two ways to lose: decrease your calories moderately (by 400–800 a day) and increase your exercise to burn more.

Exercise

Oh, no, not that dreaded word! Yep, the fact is that if you spend most of your time on the couch or at a desk, you are at risk of weight gain, a sluggish system, and depression.

"Thirty to 50 minutes of exercise up to five times a week is the healthiest thing you can do for yourself," says

Paula Papanek, Ph.D., assistant professor of physical therapy at Marquette University.

She says that few college students get enough exercise. "I remember in college thinking that I couldn't do another thing, that I was committed to the max," she says. But, she points out, exercise is preventive health maintenance and can make you more efficient and a better student in the long run if you stay healthy.

"Besides," laughs Tim, "no chicks will want to date you if you are fat and out of shape!" Seriously, he points out that keeping your self-esteem up and not having people look at you "as a total shlep" is a valid reason to exercise. "I heard the horror stories about the 'Freshman 15' and I didn't want to come home the first time and have everyone say, 'Well, I see Tim got hit with it as well.'"

Regular exercise helps in several ways:

- **Weight control.** The more calories you burn, the more you can eat. If you diet off 10 pounds, it will probably be about half fat and half muscle; if you exercise you can change that to up to 90 percent fat. Exercise not only burns calories while you are doing it, it revs up your metabolism so you burn more calories all day.

- **General improved health.** Exercise strengthens muscles including your heart, reduces blood pressure, and builds strong bones.

- **Stress management.** College is stressful, there's no doubt about that. Stress causes a bunch of hormones to be released into your bloodstream. "That makes your respiratory and heart rates go up, and makes you jumpy and jittery," says Dr. Papanek. "That's normal. It's a protective response designed to heighten your awareness so if you are threatened you can react quickly—we call it the 'fight-or-flight' response." The response becomes unhealthy when it's overwhelming, sustained, or repeated. Dr. Papanek points out that a little test anxiety is okay if it makes you study, but it's pathological if you can't sleep or eat.

Exercise directs those stress hormones into physical responses—it makes glucose available to your muscles, gets blood to where it needs to be, and releases other hormones that make you feel good. "When you are done exercising," she says, "your brain says, 'the hormones have done their job, we can go back to a healthy base line now' and it brings your body back into balance."

"When things got tense for me, I'd play basketball," Tim says. "You can always find someone to go with you because they're looking for stress relief too."

Studies show that exercise can be as helpful as drug therapy for some people in treating depression. Everybody in college has "blue" days or times when the demands seem overwhelming. A good workout can flood your brain with the hormones that are "uppers" and wash away the blues.

Do you have to become a marathon runner to get the benefits of exercise? No way. Dr. Papanek says that just taking a half-hour brisk walk with your roommate four or five times a week can be enough to make a difference. Join an intramural team too and you'll have plenty of exercise.

Here are some exercise tips:

- **Pick something you enjoy.** What's your pleasure: swimming, tennis, aerobics, karate? They're all offered at most colleges.

- **Start slowly, don't overdo it.** If you've spent most of a semester sitting on your butt, don't run five miles the first day. You may pay with an injury that can sideline you for weeks.

- **Don't compare yourself to others.** So someone else can run 10 miles; you don't have to. Do what's right for you and compare yourself to your own past performance—watch yourself get better!

- **Choose someone as an exercise buddy.** "Having someone to be accountable to helps you avoid the excuses—I've got a big test, I'm too tired," Tim says. "The next day it will be something else, so it helps to have that other person."

- **If you are going to do a sport competitively, pick someone at your own level to play with.** "If you are at opposite ends of the spectrum, one guy will be working too hard for the shape he's in and the other one will get frustrated because he's not getting a good workout," says Tim.

- **Realize that weight lifting alone isn't enough.** It may build muscles, but it doesn't increase your heart rate or build cardiovascular fitness. Include it in a balanced exercise program.

- **Always warm up first.** Picture your muscles as chewing gum—cold, they are hard and stiff; warm, they are supple. Warm muscles are less likely to be injured.

- **Wear good shoes.** Of all exercise equipment, shoes are the most important. Get shoes designed for your sport; don't run in tennis shoes. You risk injury if you wear the wrong shoes.

- **Don't discount incidental exercise.** Use the stairs instead of the elevator, park at the far end of the lot, bike to class—it's only a few minutes each time, but it adds up.

- **Spot reducing doesn't work.** All the leg lifts in the world won't remove fatty saddlebags from your thighs, situps won't peel away a spare tire without general weight reduction through eating less and exercising more.

Too much exercise can be dangerous too, especially for women, although Dr. Papanek points out that there's more operating in those cases than just exercise—the person actually develops obsessive/compulsive behavior. A warning sign for women is when the menstrual periods stop. "That's never normal," Papanek says. "It means you are in hormone imbalance, your body perceives that you don't have enough energy for reproduction and it shuts down. You're not producing enough estrogen—that can make a teenager just like a postmenopausal woman, losing bone." If your period stops, get medical help.

Eating Disorders:
When Eating Is Out of Control

Beth, whom you met at the beginning of this chapter, picked up 30 pounds when she started college. She really wanted to take it off—and she did. But then she got caught up in a vicious cycle of weight loss she couldn't control. "I discovered that all I had to do was stop eating," she remembers. Eventually, she nearly starved herself to death.

At the peak of her disease, her 5′ 7″ body was wrapped in just a few inches of flesh. At 95 pounds there was barely enough "meat" to pad her behind when she sat; every knob on every bone was visible through her papery skin. Beth had anorexia, a disease that's epidemic among college women.

"I remember sitting there hating my body, wishing I

could just chop it off," she says with a shudder of her still slim shoulders. That, says Laura Lees, Psy.D., who has been the director of an eating disorders clinic at a psychiatric hospital, is typical of a young woman with anorexia.

"Anorexia," she points out, "simply means weight loss." Anorexia nervosa is a more specific term that means a deliberate starving of the self. Anorectics (90 percent of whom are female) simply can't understand that they are too thin. In a related eating disorder, bulimia, the person gorges on huge amounts of food and then purges the body of what was eaten by throwing up, using laxatives, starvation dieting, or overexercising (especially common in males). Some experts fear that as many as 25 percent of college-aged women engage in gorging and purging.

Anorexia and bulimia are complicated disorders; many times they exist together. They usually have several causes.

The two major causes, Dr. Lees says, are societal pressure to be thin and family dysfunction. "Advertising and the media paint a picture of the perfect woman as being seriously underweight," she says. Top fashion models often weigh 25 percent less than their ideal weight. Families contribute to the disorder when children are expected to be perfect and to suppress their negative emotions.

Beth, like many young women, eventually had to be hospitalized when her weight became dangerously low. Anorectics have died when their starved heart muscle lost its normal rhythm and went into an uncontrolled flutter. Beth is one of the lucky ones; she found a therapist who could help her. Today, although she hasn't returned to college, she is building a new life for herself.

You need to know the signs of anorexia nervosa, either in yourself or in a friend:

- Excessive weight loss.
- Stubborn refusal to eat even when hungry, irritable, or lightheaded from lack of food.
- Compulsive exercise, usually a solitary activity such as running rather than a team sport.
- Inaccurate body image—saying "I'm so fat" when obviously not overweight, constant weighing—often several times a day.
- Strange rituals around food—preparing it a certain way, hiding it.
- Perfectionism in other areas—appearance, grades, relationships, sports, neatness, organization.
- "Black and white" thinking—everything is bad or good, no shades of gray.
- Change in wardrobe—dressing in layers to hide thinness, being constantly cold, wearing heavy sweaters in summer.
- Spending a lot of time in the bathroom, especially after meals. Roommates may hear vomiting, vigorously denied by the person.

If you, or a friend, display these symptoms and you suspect an eating disorder, get help. This is not something you can handle yourself. Talk to your RA, to the campus health service, if necessary call the person's parents—they can be totally unaware of what's happening. Remember that anorexia nervosa and bulimia can cause death.

Even better than treatment is prevention. Here are some tips from Dr. Lees:

- Look at how you were parented. Were your parents overly controlling? If so, give yourself permission to be an individual. While disrespect toward your parents is not God pleasing, you do have the right to become your own person. Talk to a counselor to sort out your feelings and options.

- Have interests, a way to build your self-esteem, so you won't feel your appearance defines you.

- Express your feelings. Learn to deal with anger in constructive ways instead of saying, "I shouldn't feel that way."

- Don't make food an issue. If you must diet, don't dwell on it or make it the central topic of conversation. Avoid "good foods/bad foods" labels. Don't get into a "who can lose the most" contest with your friends or roommate.

- Don't make a friend's eating or not eating a power struggle. You'll lose.

- Don't call yourself or your friends fat or tease about weight. If you or a friend are overweight, you need healthier eating patterns and more exercise not shame, blame, and crash diets.

- Feed yourself and your friends emotionally. Remind yourself of your many good qualities; tell your friends how much you care about them.

- Remember that God created your body. Bodies come in various sizes and shapes, and they're all good. Accept your body for what it is; don't require a pencil-thin shape if that's not your genetic heritage.

Healthy Sleeping Habits

Nobody needs to tell a college student to get enough sleep—if only you had the time! But there are a few tips that can help even when there don't seem to be enough hours to get everything done and sleep too.

- Resist the temptation to pull an all-nighter. The studying you do at 4:00 A.M. isn't likely to be very efficient; you'll probably do better on a test with a good night's sleep.

- Dorms can be noisy places; broken, fragmented sleep doesn't do your body much good. Try drug store ear plugs to screen out your roommate's stereo. For about $50 you can get a white noise machine—a small device that makes a whooshing sound that masks outside noises and promotes deeper sleep.

- Alcohol won't help you sleep. It may help you drop off initially, but it disrupts the normal sleep wave patterns, can cause you to wake in the middle of the night, and gives you a morning-after hangover.

- Caffeine can really destroy your ability to sleep. People who are especially sensitive may not be able to handle it after noon. And remember, it's not just coffee—soda and chocolate have it too.

- Take a nap. It worked in kindergarten, why not in college? Naps are a good way to keep up on sleep if you've got a lot to do at night. For some people, a good 20-minute nap each day is a must. Do what works for you—the key is a quiet place to let your mind and body shut down for a while to "recharge" your batteries.

Stress

We've already talked about the body's hormonal reaction to stress and the role of exercise. Here, let's look at stress more generally.

What is stress? The health dictionary says it is

demands placed on you by experiences which cause your body to become aroused to meet those demands. Stress can be either positive or negative—it's all in your perspective.

Experts say there are three stages of stress:

1. Alarm, as your body becomes aroused.
2. Resistance, as your body tries to adapt to ongoing stress.
3. Exhaustion, as your body reaches the limit of its ability to handle stress.

Obviously, you want to break the cycle before stages 2 and 3.

Factors in college that can cause stress are many: time and academic demands, competition, crowded living situations, separation from home and family, financial problems, lack of recreation, adjusting to a new area, building a social support network.

Some signs that you may be under stress include the following:

- Mood changes—irritability, fear, anger, confusion, forgetting important deadlines, difficulty concentrating, difficulty sleeping, racing mind, not being able to relax even on weekends or vacations.
- Feeling of always being rushed, never having enough time.
- Either loss of appetite or increased desire to eat.
- Muscle tightness, especially in the back and neck.
- Digestive upset—stomachache, diarrhea or constipation.
- Racing heart, rising blood pressure.
- Skin eruptions like acne or eczema.

There are some things you can do to help yourself cope with stress:

- Exercise—See the information on pages 38–42.
- Get organized. Have a schedule, a way to keep track of deadlines, regular patterns for sleeping, eating, and studying.
- Schedule regular breaks for fun and unwinding.
- Avoid getting overcommitted. Learn to say no.
- Be aware of your individual biorhythms. Try to schedule classes and study times when you are at your peak: Avoid 8:00 A.M. classes if you are a night owl, don't take late afternoon classes if you are a morning person.
- Keep physical stress to a minimum—study in a chair with decent support rather than lounging on the bed.
- Try to change your perception of stressful situations through self talk—remind yourself to keep things in proportion, that one quiz doesn't mean your entire grade, that you can get it all done by careful planning and organization.
- Try deep breathing or progressive muscle relaxation as stress busters.
- Pray. Keep close to God—He will always be there to support you.

Infectious Diseases

College is a perfect environment for germs to spread: crowded living conditions, people packed together indoors in the classroom, shared bathrooms, sometimes shared food or utensils. You can't avoid germs—they're like the armies of Attila the Hun, everywhere around you.

But by understanding a little about how infection is spread and taking some simple precautions, you can increase your chance of avoiding infection.

Some infections are caused by a virus—an incomplete submicroscopic structure that has to occupy a human cell to live. Viral illnesses include colds, influenza (the respiratory kind, not the misnamed stomach flu which can be either viral or bacterial), and many sexually transmitted diseases. The good news about viral illnesses is that most of them are self-limiting, that is, they run their course and go away. The bad news is that antibiotics don't touch them.

Other infections are caused by bacteria—microscopic organisms that can live outside the human body. Examples of bacterial illnesses include bladder infections, strep throat, food poisoning from salmonella, and secondary infections after a cold such as bronchitis or an ear infection. They can be zapped by an antibiotic.

Both viruses and bacteria are spread by direct contact, droplets in the air, and through contaminated food and water. You can't get away from these critters, but there are a few things you can do to keep from getting sick:

- Wash your hands. Mom always told you this but it's never been as important as at college. Obviously wash after using the bathroom, but it doesn't hurt to wash your hands after coming back from class or any place where there were lots of people.

- Resist the temptation for a lick of someone's ice cream. Don't use other people's glasses or utensils.

- Try to avoid getting run down—that means eating well and trying to get enough sleep. I know, it's hard. But an exhausted, undernourished body is more susceptible to infection.

A few words about mononucleosis, the college students' scourge: Mono is a mildly contagious infection caused by a virus found mostly in saliva, explains Dr. Nicholas Owen, a doctor of internal medicine. The virus seems to sit in many people's throats and we don't know why some people get sick and others don't. It seems to be spread by exchange of saliva, as in kissing (it might also be wise to watch those ice cream licks!). A person with mono can be contagious as long as a month before having symptoms, or for several months after.

For most people, mono is a minor illness with low-grade fever, sore throat, enlarged lymph nodes, and fatigue; many people think they have just a cold or the flu. Once you've had it you are usually immune; studies show that by graduation about 80 percent of college students will have had mono, most without knowing it. But in a few students the infection can be severe with an enlarged liver or spleen, and extreme fatigue lasting a long time; some students have had to drop out for a semester to recover. There's no cure—treatment involves rest and time.

"The best prevention is to get it as a child," says Dr. Owen. "But since we don't know why some people get mono and others don't, the next best prevention is general health maintenance: diet, sleep, and exercise."

Emotional Health: Depression and Suicide

Everybody gets depressed sometimes, and college students are no exception. A lot of depressing things can happen at college: work overload, poor grades, roommate problems, or the end of a relationship. Add those stresses to missing home and family and the black clouds can hang over your head.

That kind of depression is usually temporary—getting through finals week, doing well on the next test, meeting someone new, can all work a miraculous cure.

But sometimes the depression doesn't lift. It can spiral down into a true clinical depression in which the person withdraws from the people and things that usually provide support and pleasure, causing even more feelings of hopelessness and isolation. Severe depression can also be the result of a medical problem—chemical or hormone imbalance or thyroid disease.

Signs of depression include

- Losing interest in your usual activities: Sports, classes, social relationships seem dull, boring, not worth pursuing.

- Appetite switches gears—either eating too much and piling on pounds, or being unable to eat as weight drops off.

- Changes in sleep patterns. All college students prize sleep, but if your sleep pattern changes, either lying awake with persistent insomnia or sleeping hours away during the day, it can be a sign of trouble.

- Blaming yourself for everything that goes wrong in classes, in relationships, with your roommate, whether or not any of them are your fault.

- Having a negative self-image. A lot of college students struggle with fear and uncertainty, but if it reaches the point of hating yourself ("I'm *so* stupid"), it's not healthy.

- Giving off a constant air of sadness, hopelessness, or worry. Listen if friends tell you that you seem very sad or depressed.

- Inability to concentrate or pay attention. This doesn't

mean the normal distractions of college life—finding it hard to study because there's a party next door—but a true mental fog that doesn't lift.

- Aggressive behavior, especially in drinking, driving, or with weapons, or its opposite, withdrawal from social contact, excessive fearfulness.

- A constant state of restlessness, sense of being agitated with no reason.

- Physical aches and pains—headaches, backaches, neck and muscle pain, stomach upsets, constipation, diarrhea.

- Decline in schoolwork. Many college students see their grades drop a bit from high school, but A's that suddenly plummet to D's are a bad sign, especially if you can't really seem to care.

- Morbid thoughts about death—obsession with depressing literature and authors who have committed suicide.

Unrecognized depression can lead to thoughts of suicide. Every year about 100,000 young people under the age of 24 attempt suicide; 5,000 succeed, triple the rate of 30 years ago.

"Not everybody who is depressed is suicidal, but almost everybody who is suicidal is depressed," says Debra Reid, CICSW (Certified Independent Clinical Social Worker). Her private practice has included work with college students. "Sometimes it takes a professional assessment to find out what you are dealing with."

People still believe a lot of myths about suicide, she says:

- *Those who talk about it don't do it.* That's probably the most common myth and the most destructive.

Indeed, people who talk about it *do* do it.

- *People just need to look at the bright side and they'll feel better.* Pointing out all the good things in a person's life may cause added guilt instead of lifting the depression.

- *Talk about suicide, or trying it, is only a way to get attention.* Everyone wants attention, but feeling so hopeless that suicide seems the only answer is not just a craving to be noticed; it's far more serious.

- *The crisis is over when the person seems to feel better.* Not necessarily. A more cheerful outlook may mean that he or she has made a decision to commit suicide.

- *Talking about suicide will just put the idea into the person's head.* If someone is feeling desperate, asking if he or she is thinking about suicide won't put anything into his or her head that isn't already there. Having the feeling confronted may be a real relief.

- *People who commit suicide are mentally ill.* Some are, but many aren't. Some are just so overwhelmed with stress and pain they don't know how to cope.

What drives a person to make the terrible choice to end his or her life? Many times, says Reid, people who make an attempt don't really intend to die. "They intend to stop the pain," she says. "They want that pain that they feel so eaten by to stop and they don't know how else to do that."

There are, Reid says, some factors which put a person at higher risk for suicide:

- A prior attempt.
- A family member or close friend who has committed suicide.
- A "family lifestyle" of depression—some families

53

have a history of depression; it may be genetic or behavioral.

- Drug and alcohol use can make a chemical imbalance worse or intensify aggressive feelings.
- Unsettled sexual identity—feeling unattractive, fearful of being homosexual, or afraid of sexual feelings.
- A dramatic change in family life, especially divorce or remarriage.
- A great deal of stress and limited coping skills—academic pressure, financial problems, rejection by friends, end of a romance.
- A pattern of violent or aggressive behavior, engaging in dangerous activities, having brushes with the law or the other extreme, a pattern of shyness and isolation.
- Physical or sexual abuse by a family member, trusted friend or acquaintance, especially for women.
- Rigid, black-and-white thinking patterns.
- Clinical depression or mental illness.

Signs to Watch for

According to Reid, signs of suicidal tendencies include the signs of depression plus

- A person making an attempt to harm himself physically, no matter how minor.
- Making threats, saying things like "I just don't think I can take it any more" or "if I weren't here, things would be better."
- Preoccupation with death: Talking, writing, drawing pictures, watching movies about it, unhealthy occupation with symbols or objects representing it, reading books by authors who have committed suicide.

- Withdrawal from family, friends, and normal activities.
- Violent, rebellious behavior: Playing with weapons, breaking the law, explosive outbursts.
- Abusing drugs and alcohol.
- Giving away things she loves such as favorite clothing, a stereo set, books, or CDs.
- An unexplained "high" or cheerful mood after a period of depression—this may be a signal that he has decided on suicide and made a plan.
- Suicide of a friend or admired celebrity.

The actual attempt is often precipitated by a painful or humiliating event. Sometimes it can be something as common as the breakup of a romance. Not making a team, getting a bad grade, or failing a course can set it off. In these days of high college costs, losing a job needed to pay the bills or losing a scholarship because of low grades can be devastating. An encounter with the law or being a crime victim (especially of sexual assault) can set off suicidal thoughts.

When a Friend Is Depressed

What if it's somebody else rather than yourself you are worried about? According to Beverly Yahnke, Ph.D., a therapist in private practice, having a depressed friend or roommate is not uncommon during college years. "It can be one of the most discouraging and depressing circumstances for college students," she says. "Your sleep and study time can be interrupted, you can be worried all the time to the point of taking responsibility for another person's life. That's not a healthy situation. You can't have a normal college experience if you become the caretaker of another young adult."

What should you do?

- Don't assume that every blue day your roommate has is a real depression. On the other hand, if he or she is showing many of the signs of depression listed earlier in this chapter, trust your instincts. If you think something unhealthy is going on, you could very well be right.

- If your friend or roommate is making threats or giving verbal warnings, don't assume he or she is just kidding. Listen closely; evaluate carefully.

- Take into account any crisis the friend has experienced such as the death of a parent, suicide of a friend, romantic breakup, flunking a course, or losing a scholarship.

- Be supportive. Tell your friend you care and you don't want him or her to do anything stupid, harmful, or permanent.

- If you've got drugs, alcohol, or anything else dangerous in your room, get rid of them.

- Don't be afraid to ask a direct question: "Are you thinking about suicide?" "Have you done anything about it?"

- Don't leave a seriously depressed or suicidal person alone.

- You must get help. You cannot become the person's caretaker. You don't have the knowledge or experience to do that. Your RA or campus counseling service is a good place to start. Call your parents if you can't find help; sometimes the college will listen more readily to an adult than a student.

- If your friend's situation is life-threatening, if he or she has done something harmful or is trying to, notify your RA immediately. If you can't reach the RA, take the person to an emergency room.

There are a few things you should *not* do:

- A promise to keep depression or suicidal thoughts secret makes things worse. It's better for a person to lose trust for a little while than to end up dead.

- Acting shocked or panicked may make the person more panicked himself. It's hard to stay calm, but that's what your friend needs.

- Making judgmental statements about all suicides going to hell won't help. Emphasize that God hears our voices crying from the depths (Psalm 130). He forgives *all* our sins and doesn't keep a record of them. What great news that is! Tell the person that it's not wrong to feel depressed but our hope is in Christ, through whom we have forgiveness and eternal life.

Depression is not a hopeless illness. It can be helped with therapy and, sometimes, medication. The sooner the better.

"A student with deep problems needs special help," says Dr. Yahnke. "You can't become a psychiatric nurse no matter how much you care." That's why, she emphasizes, you need to get help both for yourself in handling such a situation and for your friend.

Does it sound like college is harmful to your health? Not true—with wise choices and a positive outlook you can stay healthy both physically and emotionally and get the most out of your college experience.

3

Guy/Girl Relationships, Dating, and—*Gulp*—Sexual Pressure

All the Dating Rules Have Gone Out the Window

So says Katie, who, at the beginning of her senior year in college, has gradually worked her way into the college dating scene. It's not like high school, she says. It's not necessarily the social whirl movies and novels would have you believe. College dating can be great fun and can lead to a lasting relationship, but it can also hold danger.

Let's look at the world of college dating through the eyes of some students who have been there, done that.

What's a College "Date" Really Like?

Most students are broke most of the time; for many, college is more or less a life of perpetual poverty. That, says Katie, is probably the biggest factor in dictating what people do on dates. Formal dates in which the guy does the asking and treats the woman to dinner and a movie are rare, she points out. "It does happen, but most college students can't afford it," she says.

Instead, campus dates are likely to be going for a walk or bike ride, in-line skating, getting coffee, studying together, going to a college sports event, or—most popular of all—renting a movie and watching it in someone's room. And, of course, there are always parties and barhopping.

Even when a date does involve some expense, such as movie admission or a meal out, it's no longer assumed that the guy will pay all the bills, Katie says. Most often people split the bill or take turns paying. That makes it easier on everyone's wallet, but it also, according to Katie, prevents a feeling that the woman "owes" the man something because he's paid the bills.

College parties need a bit of explanation, Katie says. There are two kinds: parties that require an invitation and those that are open to anyone. Open parties are often sponsored by a club, fraternity, or house full of students to make money. You buy a cup at the door and that entitles you to unlimited beer or alcoholic punch for the night. "Sometimes they pack 300 people into the basement of a house," she says. "It sure wasn't my scene!"

That kind of party can be a place to meet people (although Katie says the type of people she met weren't necessarily the ones she wanted to spend time with), but they also can have serious consequences. If you are under the legal drinking age and you are caught at such a party, you could be in big trouble with the law even if you weren't drinking. If you are over 21, there's a huge temptation to drink too much when you can just refill your cup over and over again. If you are of legal age and you plan to go to such a party, you'd be wise to decide in advance how much you're going to drink and stick to it.

Getting Started—
How Do You Meet People?

Some kids didn't date a lot in high school but would like a more active social life in college. How do you get started?

Katie says the best way is the same way you get started making friends—by being friendly. The first couple of weeks, she confesses, she was so intimidated by the new world of college that she mainly went to class and curled up in her room. After a couple of weeks she realized that she'd have to reach out if she wanted to have friends.

"I started by saying hi to the other girls on my floor and getting to know them," she says. "I met a lot of other people through them. Then I made myself start talking to the people around me in class and everywhere else I went. Pretty soon I was known as a friendly person." Gradually her circle of acquaintances grew, she made some real friends, and she began dating a few guys.

To meet people to date, go to places where there are people with common interests, she says. If you're looking for an academic type, try the library. If you're interested in a jock, work out at the fitness center. There's always church, student government, interest clubs, and classes—which change every semester—offering a whole new group of potential dates. Most of the guys Katie dated she met in class, the premed club, dorm activities, and the campus religious center. She didn't find bars a very good place to meet people. Parties are okay, she says, but you have to be very careful.

Women also have to be willing to call guys they are interested in. "If you sit around waiting for him to call you, it may never happen," Katie says. "It's not at all uncommon now for a girl to call a guy."

One good thing about the campus social scene, she says, is that there's less emphasis on appearance. "Individuality is valued more than it was in high school," she says. "You don't have to dress in the latest fashions—people appreciate you for how you dress to be yourself." You can pick out the people who buy the latest fashion magazines and dress from them, she says, but most students live in jeans, T-shirts, and sweatshirts. "It's a relief not to have to plan what you are going to wear or to be sure you don't wear the same thing twice in one week like in high school," she laughs.

A Few Words about the Boyfriend or Girlfriend You Left Behind

For a lot of kids starting college there's an additional adjustment because they are leaving behind a boyfriend or girlfriend from high school. Some of those relationships are very intense and it can be hard to say goodbye. Often the goodbyes are accompanied by promises to write or call every day, not to date anyone else, to "be true" to each other. And those promises can certainly be sincere, from the heart.

If you are leaving behind a high school love, you don't want to hear this, but the fact is that most high school relationships don't survive the separation of college. A few do. Mine was one of them—I married my high school boyfriend after four years of being in different colleges. It can happen. Most often it doesn't.

For Kristin it didn't. Her boyfriend left for college

while she stayed behind for her last year of high school. The relationship hung on through Christmas, but then faded away. "College and high school are just two different worlds," Kristin reflects. "We were used to being in the same world, but now it was completely different for him—different pressures, different things he was being offered. The person staying behind may try to understand, but you can't because you haven't experienced it, and that puts a lot of stress on you and on the relationship. The other person changes and grows in different ways, is surrounded by different friends you don't know, does things you've never done. When you try to tell him or her what you've been doing, it's something they've already done. They're beyond that and on to new and better things. You are just left behind."

Kristin was on the other side a year later when she left for college and her new boyfriend didn't. Many of the same factors came into play. "He wasn't experiencing the same things I was either in academics or in the social world. I was meeting so many interesting new people. Often the person left behind becomes possessive, the one away is building new relationships and he or she isn't part of it. The other person can become jealous of the new people, even those of the same sex. He or she is afraid of losing the other person, and in the majority of cases that's what happens." That relationship died within a few months also.

If you have a relationship you are leaving behind, here are a few suggestions:

- Expect that you will miss the other person—a lot. More than a few tears have been shed saying goodbye as well as from the blues of missing each other. That's normal. But don't let your blue mood infect your whole life. If you sit in your dorm room wallowing in your misery, you will miss much of the fun of college. The antidote to the blues is getting out, meeting people, having fun. Besides, your letters and phone calls will be much more interesting if you can share some fun things you've done rather than dwelling on your sadness.

- It's wise not to make promises you might not be able to keep. Vowing to never go out with anyone else may not be smart if you and your significant other are far apart and won't see each other often. An agreement that casual dating is okay for both of you may give you the freedom to have fun at college and be sure the other person is really right for you.

- If you agree not to see anyone else, then you have to have a great deal of trust and confidence between you. Jealousy, trying to find out if the other person is "cheating," accusations, and sleepless nights won't deepen your relationship. They will probably destroy it.

- Little, thoughtful things can help. Notes, little presents, quick phone calls, e-mail messages—"I'm thinking about you"—can bridge long distances, especially if you know the other person is going through some kind of crisis.

- If the other person is close by, be careful that you don't spend every weekend with him or her and never become part of your own campus. There's more to college than getting an education. It's also the friends you make, the growing and maturing you do. If you tie yourself to another person, going home to him or her every weekend, you may give up a lot of what college has to offer.

- If your boyfriend or girlfriend comes with you to the

same school, you have an entirely different challenge. If you spend every minute together, eating all your meals together, studying together, and going to every activity as a pair, you may not meet other people or make new friends. That can be devastating if the relationship breaks up later. Everyone else will have formed friendship groups and you might find it much harder to make friends than you would have at the beginning of the year.

Sexual Pressure

"Nobody believes I never have!" Jon leans back, stretches out his long legs and laughs. "No matter how many times I say it, nobody believes it. 'Sure, whatever' is the usual response."

He recalls one young woman he was dating who asked him how many people he'd had sex with. "Why don't you guess," he challenged her.

"Well, I'd say … seven."

"No."

"Eight?"

"Wrong way."

She worked her way down to one.

"No. I haven't had sex with anyone."

"She couldn't get over it," Jon says. "But I don't care. I'll tell girls right out, 'I'm not going to have sex with you.' If they don't like it, fine. If they do—then that's fine too."

Most girls are surprised, he says. A few have stopped dating him because of it. But many are relieved.

National statistics say that 75 percent of freshman have sex before they come to college and the number hits 90 percent by the time graduation day rolls around. Whether you believe those numbers or not, sex is a big feature of campus life today.

David Lipsky, writing in *Rolling Stone* magazine (March 23, 1995), describes a campus scene that has chilling implications: A bunch of guys are sitting around a fraternity house drinking beer. One jumps to his feet and shouts to his "brothers," asking if they'll have sex with an "ugly chick." They shout back, "Yes!" The speaker later explained to Lipsky that he'd take some ribbing the morning after he'd had sex with an "ugly chick," but it was worth it because he'd had sex. And, ultimately, he'd get respect from his friends too. That's what mattered most to him: sex and the approval of his peers.

That story says a lot of things about campus attitudes toward sex, none of them very good. It illustrates how women are often seen as sex objects and judged for their appearance. It shows male attitudes about what makes a guy a "man." It turns a powerful spotlight on the attitude that sex is not a beautiful expression of love between two people committed to each other for life in marriage, but is a game. Recreation. A power trip. And while that story is about one specific frat party, the attitude it represents can be found on most any campus.

You are going to meet that attitude in college. And it won't be subtle, it will be in your face.

Katie says the most pressure she's ever gotten about her decision not to have sex until marriage came, surprisingly, from another young woman. "There were seven or eight girls sitting around in a dorm room freshman year and the conversation turned to sex," she remembers. "Everyone started talking about their sexual experiences and I had none to report. One girl just attacked me, 'How can you do that? Why would anyone want to be with you if you have no experience and don't know what you are doing? How can you vow to be with someone for the rest of your life if you don't know if you are sexually compatible?' She was just going nuts!"

Perhaps the young woman's overreaction was because she felt guilty about what she was doing and had to justify it. Or, perhaps she had really bought the line that if you don't have sex, there's something wrong with you. Either way her reaction is sad: She's casually squandering the greatest gift one person can give another—the sharing of your whole self.

In God's plan, sex is reserved for two people who are committed to each other and have formalized that commitment in marriage. The problem you will face is finding the resolve to stick to that plan in the sexual stew of today's college campus.

Despite all the media promotion of sexual freedom, despite the attitudes of many college students, the fact is there *are* people on every campus who *aren't* having sex, who are saving that gift for their future spouses. They may not talk about it as freely as Jon and Katie, but they're there. "I just wish they wore a label so I could find them," Katie laughs.

But there are no labels. The best thing you can do, Katie says, is to stand up for what you believe and find your friends, and ultimately your dates, from among people who have the same values as you. "I avoid sexual pressure by dating people with values like mine," Katie says. "Guys know what I stand for right from the start so I don't tend to have a problem."

She's very open about telling people, including dates, that she doesn't intend to have sex until marriage, Katie says. "Guys' eyes get kind of big when I say that," she says, "but most of them have kept dating me, they didn't drop me because of it. I've had a few put pressure on me—'I just want to show you how much I care about you'—but that was the end of that relationship."

Katie says that many of the young women she's met at college have told her they regret becoming sexually active. One friend became pregnant during her freshman year, dropped out to have the baby, gave it up for adoption, and returned to college. "I wish I had done what you are doing," she told Katie. "I wish I had thought about it more. I really regret it now."

You don't even have to get pregnant to regret having sex, she points out. Several young women have confided to her that they wanted their first sexual experience to be special and it wasn't. It wasn't with the right person, it wasn't at the right time, they weren't mature enough to handle it, and they didn't stay with the guy. "A lot of guys use girls, then the girls regret it when the guy moves on," Katie says. "The best way to avoid regret is to come to a firm decision not to have sex until marriage. It just makes things so much easier—I don't have to worry about all the things that sexually active people have to worry about."

"Some people see that decision as being stubborn and narrow-minded," Jon says, "but other people see it as standing up for what you believe in." Believe it or not, you will get respect from many people for having firm values and standing up for them, he says.

The Frightening World of Date Rape

College can be a dangerous place for a woman. "Date rape is a significant problem on most college campuses," says Dr. Andrew Luptak, vice president of student life at Concordia University, Wisconsin, who wrote the date rape prevention program *Honoring One Another* used at all the Concordia universities. "It may be somewhat exaggerated in the press, but it is a significant problem," he says.

He shares some statistics that he has gathered from various researchers:

- 20–25 percent of college women experience some sort of forced sexual contact during their college years.
- 15 percent of men report having unwilling sexual contact.
- 90 percent of date rapes go unreported.
- According to the FBI, women between the ages of 16 and 24 are at the highest risk for sexual assault.
- College athletes are charged with sexual assault at a far greater rate than other college men.

There's an underlying societal attitude that allows sexual assault, Dr. Luptak says, and that's the "boys will be boys" viewpoint. "It starts in the home, it's how people are raised and what things are tolerated," he says. "I believe that our schools, from elementary through college, haven't done an effective job of teaching students how to interact with one another. From little on people are not told, 'That's inappropriate behavior and this is how you should act.'"

According to Mary Rouse, dean of students at the University of Wisconsin, Madison, the vast majority of date rapes involve alcohol: Either one or both of the parties is drunk and not thinking clearly. "We often see situations where students are dating; you add alcohol to the mix and, all of a sudden, it's out of control," she says. "The effects can be devastating."

The fact that one or both of the people involved were drunk *never* excuses rape. But while date rape is always the fault of the aggressor and not the victim, women need to understand that drinking to excess and being out of control is a really *dumb* thing to do.

Here, from Dr. Luptak, Mary Rouse, and some other experts, are some tips for women for lowering the risk of being raped on a date:

- Think about your standards in advance. Know your own limits and make sure any men you date are aware of them too. Learn to say **no** loudly and clearly. "Women need to be assertive," says Dr. Luptak.

- Be sure you aren't giving off mixed messages—in the way you dress, the way you act (flirting is fun, but sending a message of sexual availability is risky), in the amount you drink.

- If a man has a pattern of putting down women, he's probably bad news. If he tells lots of sexual jokes and makes comments that demean women, he probably doesn't respect women. Men who don't respect women are unlikely to stop when women say no.

- In a similar way, if a man wants to control you and everything you do, he's probably not good date material. There are men who think they should be in charge, who want to control every aspect of their girlfriends' lives and their relationships. That kind of man often thinks he's entitled to run the sexual part of the relationship also. Remember, you have the right to be treated by a man as his equal even if your roles are different and to have your thoughts, opinions, and needs respected.

- Be leery of men who use physical power to get their way. Any man who grabs you, shoves you around, uses his body to block you, or touches you when you say no is sending bad signals. Listen to them.

- Don't leave a party or group activity with a guy, especially to go to a secluded area, unless you know him *very* well. Going alone with someone to his room is taking a huge risk, especially if either of you has been drinking.

- Don't drink on a date if you are under age. If you are legal age, don't drink to the point where you don't know what you are doing. Don't go anywhere with a guy who has been drinking. Alcohol, as Mary Rouse pointed out, is the biggest single factor in rape. One college student said that her college sponsored a program on date rape. Some of the men argued that having sex with a woman who was too drunk to resist wasn't rape because she was "asking for it." That's frightening. If you are drinking, you can't think clearly, and you might not be aware of danger signals a man is sending out.

- Sexy clothes are not smart. The way a woman is dressed is never an excuse for rape, but let's face it, you do send off signals by your dress. Your clothes speak volumes about you—they make an impression. Be sure it's the impression you want to make. Think about the gift God gave you in your body, and how He would want you to use it.

A few words to guys:

College society, especially fraternity society, says that real men are the sexual aggressors; they are to be tough, macho, and above all, always ready to have sex. That's not the message God set out in His Word. Listen to what He says about sexual responsibility and how men are to relate to women.

- God says sex is for marriage only. If you remember that one simple rule, you won't even have to think about situations where sex is right or wrong. You'll have the answer.

- Pushing a woman into having sex is called **rape**. It doesn't matter how many times you've dated her, how she's dressed, how much she's had to drink, or that she agreed to come to your room.

- Stop when a woman says *no*. Immediately. She doesn't owe you anything, she doesn't really "want it" even though she's saying no. It's a myth that all women secretly want to be forced, that they find rape exciting. They find it terrifying.

- Aggressive male behavior has no place in a Christian man's life. Intimidating women by touching, pushing, blocking them, or putting them down with ugly sexist jokes is wrong. Women are your equals despite different life roles. When tempted to aggressive behavior, think of your mother or sister—would you want a man treating her that way?

- Close your ears to peer pressure. *Not* everyone is having sex. There isn't something wrong with you if you aren't "getting any."

- Remember that rape can happen to men too. It's not common, but college men have been sexually assaulted by other men. The following cautions, although written to women, also apply to men.

If It Happens to You

- Trust your instincts. If something doesn't seem quite right to you, don't just shrug it off. Get out of there. If you feel that something's wrong, it probably is.

- Stay calm, difficult as it may be. You will think more clearly if you are in control.

- Act immediately. If you don't get out of the situation right away, he may try it again. Even if you think you might be misunderstanding what he's doing, don't take a chance.

- Be assertive. Shout *No! Stop! Don't do that!* loudly and clearly. Pleading or crying will only make him feel more powerful.

- Run, screaming for help.

- If you decide to fight, do it with all your might. Rape is about anger and power, not sex. You will only make your rapist angry—and put yourself in even more danger—if you fight back halfheartedly. A self-defense course can teach you what to do—they are offered on many college campuses. Fighting is not a good choice if you've never had a self-defense class. Never fight if the rapist has a weapon. If you sense that he's really dangerous, especially if he has a weapon, it may be better to submit than to be hurt or killed.

- Some women have escaped rape by telling the rapist they have AIDS or some other sexually transmitted disease. However, this may make the rapist angry. He may still try to hurt you.

- *Tell someone.* Don't keep it to yourself. Rape is not your fault. Tell your RA, the director of student life, or a campus pastor.

- Go to the police. It may be hard, but if the rapist gets away with it, he'll probably attack someone else.

- Get medical help right away. Don't "clean up" first. You will need to be tested for sexually transmitted diseases. The police will need evidence of the rape (sperm and hair samples and other signs of forced intercourse) to bring a case against the rapist. Doctors and nurses at rape centers or the staff at your college health center will help you.

- Get some support. You may need to see a counselor for a while. Depression often follows rape, and it will be easier to deal with if you have a support system. It is possible to heal, but don't try to do it alone.

- Pray. Jesus is the ultimate source of help. Don't worry if you don't know what to pray: "The Spirit helps us in our weakness. We do not know what we ought to pray for, but the Spirit Himself intercedes for us with groans that words cannot express" (Romans 8:26).

Many colleges and universities today have rape prevention programs, either voluntary or mandatory. Some include information on date rape within the curriculum. "I think they can work," says Dr. Luptak. However, he points out, many college women who have been raped refuse to press charges, especially against athletes. That, he says, is a mistake. Women need to take responsibility and press charges so other women won't face the same thing.

There are, of course, other consequences to campus sex, including unwanted pregnancy and sexually transmitted diseases. We'll look at some of those risks in the next chapter.

Dating can be a wonderful part of college life. Many people have found their life partner at college; others, while not necessarily finding the person they want to marry, have learned a lot about themselves and what they are looking for in a mate. That's all part of what you've gone to college to learn.

Enjoy the dating game, remember the place of sex in the life of a child of God, and know that God is there to support and protect you. Live your college life so you can look back on those dating days with joy, not with pain and regret. That's the best gift you can give yourself.

4

College Can Be a Dangerous Place

Knowing the Risks of Alcohol, Drugs, and Promiscuity

The morning Lisa woke up with her head in a garbage can was the morning she finally asked herself, "Why am I doing this? Is this really fun?"

Lisa didn't drink at all in high school. When she went to college—alone, not knowing anyone—she really wanted a social life. "The first few weekends I was alone, the dorms were empty because everyone was off at some kind of a party," she says. "If you wanted any kind of a social life, you had to go along."

She wanted friends, she wanted to be accepted, so she went along.

"You could always find a party," she recalls. "You'd pay $2.00 at the door for a cup and you could drink your fill of beer—always cheap, awful beer!" (Sometimes, as an alternative, it's punch, usually a lethal mixture of grape juice and every kind of alcohol known to man).

Lisa didn't even like the taste of beer, but that's what

the others were drinking, so that's what she drank. She never got really plastered, she says, just "buzzed," but some of her friends quickly turned into problem drinkers. At every party they'd end up getting completely drunk, passing out, and waking up in the morning in some guy's room missing their underwear. As the person who drank the least, Lisa often fell into the role of baby-sitter for drunk friends. "I'd try to watch out for them, but you can't say to someone, 'No, you can't go home with this guy,'" she says.

While usually not as drunk as her friends were, she still recalls being buzzed to the point of vulnerability. "If something had happened," she says, "I wouldn't have been in very good shape to defend myself."

Every Monday morning, she recalls, everyone's conversation revolved around how drunk they had gotten the previous weekend and what they had done or couldn't remember doing. By the middle of the week the conversations turned to what parties people were planning to attend the coming weekend and how much they were going to drink. It quickly became incredibly boring.

Then came a party at which Lisa let her guard down and got really drunk. "I drank three two-liter wine coolers, a few shots of Yukon Jack, and a couple of beers," she says. "My friends basically piggy-backed me back to the dorm. I was with it enough to know not to sleep on my back so I wouldn't throw up and choke, so I slept with my head hanging over the side of my bed in the garbage can in case I got sick. That's how I woke up the next morning—head in the garbage."

That's when Lisa asked herself what she was doing. The image of herself haunted her. She thought about what God must think. She vowed to stop drinking. And she did.

For the next couple of months she was lonely. "Not drinking left a big hole in my life," she says. "My friends lost interest in me because I wasn't *fun* anymore. I'd sit in the dorm on Friday and Saturday nights, just me and the TV, waiting for the weekend to be over."

We'll come back to how Lisa solved that problem later in this chapter. For now, let's look at what her experience says about one of the greatest dangers in college life.

Alcohol and the College Social Scene

Alcohol is ever-present on college campuses. "I've worked in a college since the late 1960s and throughout that period alcohol has been, and continues to be, the number one drug of choice on college campuses," says Mary Rouse, dean of students at the University of Wisconsin, Madison, a school well known for its "party" atmosphere. (Note that she used the word "drug." Alcohol, which has a chemical effect on the brain, is indeed a drug.) "Yes," she continues, "there is a serious problem on this campus, across the state, and around the country."

Her opinion is backed up by the results of a Harvard School of Public Health survey of over 175,000 students at 140 different four-year colleges in 40 states. The surveyors tried to get some idea of how many American college students indulge in binge drinking, defined for males as having five or more drinks in a row once or more in a two-week period or, for females, four drinks in the same time frame.

The study turned up some horrifying statistics:

- 44 percent of college students are binge drinkers. Nearly 20 percent binge frequently, at least three or more times in two weeks. Nationally, that means three million college students are binge drinkers.

- Binge drinking is highest among students who live in fraternity or sorority houses.
- Despite all the education about drunk driving, half of binge drinkers in the study had ridden with a driver who was drunk and 40 percent of the males who were bingers admitted to driving a car after five or more drinks.

"We've known about the drinking problems on campus for many years," says Mary Rouse, "but this study lends scientific research credibility to what we already knew. Trouble never starts until the abuse of alcohol begins and then there is *always* trouble."

And don't think you are safe from the pressure to drink if you are attending a religious college. Nathan, who spent one year at a state university and then transferred to a private, religious college found he didn't leave the party atmosphere behind when he moved. "I found there was more drinking at the private school than there was at the state university," he says. "I was really surprised."

Note that we are talking about *abuse* of alcohol—using it to excess. It is possible to attend a party, have a drink, and have fun. Know your limits—and the law—and live within them.

Rouse points out that abusing alcohol puts students in danger in many ways:

- It's possible to die from alcohol poisoning. It happens every year on some campus—a student drinks too much, lapses into a coma, and even if friends take him to a hospital emergency room, he dies. Or, they put her to bed and in the morning find her dead, choked on her vomit.
- Accidents are much more likely when good judgement is alcohol-blunted. Car crashes are one exam-

ple; your life can be ended or forever changed in a moment of screeching metal and shattering glass. Other accidents can maim or kill. On my son's campus, a student who had been drinking at the bars across the river decided to swim back instead of taking the footbridge. He drowned. A student at another university, in an alcohol-sodden sleep, rolled off his loft bed and died. Drunk students have fallen out of windows, off balconies, down steps, or cracked their heads open in bathrooms.

- Alcohol fuels violence. Fist fights, verbal aggression, date rape, vandalism—alcohol usually underlies the ugliness.

- Alcohol reduces sexual inhibitions. Lisa's friends who woke in a strange room and staggered home not knowing what they had done are a prime example. "When you are drunk, guys look better than they are," she says. "My roommates would sleep with somebody and the next day he wouldn't give her the time of day when they passed in the hall." Lest you think only guys are guilty, women also talk men into doing things under the influence of alcohol that they wouldn't otherwise do. And with that kind of casual sex comes a terrible risk of sexually transmitted disease or unwanted pregnancy.

- Too much partying can lay waste to schoolwork. The academic pressures of college can be fierce; many students have washed out in a flood of alcohol. You can be expelled for alcohol-related offenses; schools take underage drinking seriously.

- If you are underage, an arrest can give you a criminal record that can follow you for years and prevent you from getting certain jobs or getting into graduate school. Even if you are legal age, if you give alcohol to someone underage, you could be looking at jail time.

Besides the horrors you can inflict on yourself with alcohol, think about what it does to others. The Harvard survey spoke of "secondhand" effects from drinking on nondrinking students: physical assault, sexual assault, impaired sleep and study time, the unpleasantness of having to clean up a roommate's vomit. The majority of college students, 87 percent in the survey, said they had experienced problems because of someone else's drinking. On some campuses nondrinking students have become militant, demanding that the school do something about the problems other people's drinking causes them.

Why do so many college students, especially new ones, get so heavily into the drinking scene? There are several reasons, says Dr. Andrew Luptak:

- **Wanting to feel grown up.** "Drinking defines you as a mature person," he says. "Mature people drink, I'm in college, I want to show I'm mature, therefore I'll drink."

- **Drinking is a way to meet people.** Remember Lisa who had no social life without drinking? Parties where students can meet each other have great appeal.

- **The campus culture.** Kids think, "I'm here to have fun. To have fun you are supposed to drink." Drinking has become a rite of passage. When surveyed about how much drinking goes on at their individual colleges, Luptak says, students usually overestimate. They really believe that everybody is doing it, when, in fact, about 20 percent of students don't drink at all.

- **Advertising.** "Look at how the media portrays alcohol use on TV, in movies, and magazines," says Luptak. "It says, 'In order to be cool, to be successful, you have to drink.' That comes at college students very hard."

Those are some of the horrors. The question is, what do you do? How do you fit into college life without alcohol? There some things you can do to make it easier.

- First, and most important, think through the issue. Think about what God says about obeying the laws of the society we live in and about the responsibility He has given us to take care of our bodies. Decide *for yourself* what your response to drinking pressure will be. Realize that if you are underage, drinking at all means you are breaking the law and it puts you at risk of the consequences. If you are legal age, decide for yourself if you choose to use alcohol and, if you do, *know your limit.* Don't ever allow yourself to be in a position where somebody else is making your decisions for you.

- If you are legal age and know you will have some alcohol at a party, go with a buddy. Make a prior agreement to look out for each other, go together, and come home together. "A caring community, a culture of connectedness will help," says Mary Rouse.

- Don't be afraid to say no. Rouse thinks a flat statement, "Thanks, but no thanks," is best. If you are pressured, she suggests you respond by saying, "I'm my own person, I make my own choices, I choose not to." Some people carry around a cup of beer or ginger ale that looks like a drink just to avoid the hassle. "I know students whose cup of beer becomes hot in their hands!" she says. She'd rather you be honest but, she says, if you are in control of your choices and it works for you, go for it.

- Try out the campus nonalcohol events. Every school has them: Parties with volleyball, DJs for dancing, pizza, everything but alcohol. "We get 1,000 kids at some of those events," Rouse says. Some schools even have on-campus, nonalcohol bars.

- If your school offers substance-free housing, give it a try. It's easier not to drink when the room you live in or the one next door isn't awash in alcohol.

- Last, but far from least, take a lesson from Lisa's experience. After several weeks of sitting alone in the dorm, she was invited to a party sponsored by a campus Christian group. "I suddenly realized there was another choice on a weekend besides going to a drinking party," she says. "I found I had fun with these people—it was a blast!" The group sponsored constant activities; sometimes they would join up with other Christian groups for even bigger events. "Get involved right away, build a group of friends that aren't into the party scene," she advises. "If somebody doesn't walk up to you, there are ways to find out—there are flyers everywhere, ask around. You'll get to know people and have fun."

Other Drugs

Alcohol is certainly the number one drug on campus—it's the elephant while other drugs are the mosquitos, Mary Rouse says—but that doesn't mean that other drugs don't exist.

Both Rouse and Dr. Luptak say they have seen an upsurge in marijuana use on their campuses in the last two or three years.

While many students feel marijuana is harmless, the truth is that it can have adverse consequences. "It causes inattentiveness, lack of ability to concentrate, impaired memory," Luptak says. "All the things that are important to academic success are the problems with marijuana."

Even more important is the illegal nature of the drug and the culture you have to deal with to obtain it, says Rouse. A student who was selling marijuana from his dorm room was recently shot to death on her campus. "There's the possibility of a criminal record, the potential risk to your academic record," she says. "There's a certain antisocial dimension to smoking marijuana in which you get separated, disconnected from society."

Other drugs may be found on campus, but less commonly. LSD, a dangerous drug that causes hallucinations and flashbacks after use, is reappearing at many schools. Other so-called "designer drugs" may be available. Neither Luptak nor Rouse sees cocaine or heroin as a big campus problem, but Rouse warns that dabbling in either of those drugs means dealing with a *very* dangerous culture. "What you have to do to get those drugs certainly puts you at risk," she warns.

Obviously there's only one response if you are offered an illegal drug at college. "Stay away," warns Luptak. "Why would you want that false feeling a drug gives you with all the medical evidence that drugs do harm to your body and can adversely affect your life?"

God expects us as Christians to obey the laws of society. Smoking marijuana or using other drugs is breaking the law. God also expects us to take good care of the bodies He has given us. Marijuana and other drugs can seriously harm your body. We cannot keep the Law perfectly by ourselves; Jesus kept it for us. It is the good news of what Jesus did for us that is our motivation to live a life that is God-pleasing. As Paul told the Romans: "I am not ashamed of the gospel, because it is the power of God for the salvation of everyone who believes. ... For in the gospel a righteousness from God is revealed, a righteousness that is by faith from first to last" (Romans 1:16–17).

The Consequences of Promiscuous Sex

If you read my book *Steer Clear: A Christian Guide to Teen Temptations*, you will remember Jenny, the young woman who spoke so movingly of what too-early parenthood had done to her life. Her story speaks especially to college students since she was in college when it happened. If you haven't read *Steer Clear*, I'll briefly review Jenny's situation. Keep her story in mind as you make important choices about the role of sex in your life.

Jenny was in her first semester of college when she met a young man, also a student. She thought he was the person she wanted to spend her life with. They had dated for a few weeks when she and the young man began thinking about expressing their feelings. "Expressing feelings" in college terminology most often means having sex. He really wanted to, she wasn't sure.

But, she reasoned, almost all her friends had already "done it." Having sex was the most popular topic for late-night dorm discussions. Women who hadn't experienced sex were subtly made to feel that perhaps there was something wrong with them—after all, why shouldn't they experience the pleasure that everybody else seemed to be having? She decided to go ahead, but insisted on using a condom.

While many college romances do turn into lasting love, many others don't. As is often the case, Jenny's relationship didn't survive. A few weeks after the breakup,

Jenny saw a chart in her biology textbook showing the failure rate for condoms in preventing pregnancy and sexually transmitted diseases. According to statistics, it ranges from 20 percent (if the condom was used correctly, every time) to 60 percent (if it wasn't used correctly or every time).

Jenny felt her stomach drop. She'd believed what she'd been told in high school biology: If you use a condom, you're safe. But the information came too late. A few days later Jenny found out she was pregnant.

She thought briefly about abortion but because she was a Christian, she decided she couldn't do it—a fortunate decision in light of the significant aftereffects many women experience after having an abortion. She also decided that she didn't want to give her child up for adoption, even though that can be a good option for the child. She knew there was no chance that she and her boyfriend would get back together, and she recognized that he wasn't good husband or father material, so she began walking the long, difficult road of parenthood alone.

Jenny's life is now very different from what she thought being a college student would be like. "Imagine how hard it would be to raise a child alone," she says. "It's at least 10 times harder."

Living in a dorm and enjoying the college social scene is obviously not possible. She's moved into a small apartment above her mother's apartment. But that's only the beginning of the changes.

She's had to get a job to support herself and her son. That meant dropping to part-time student status. She's way behind the friends she started college with—they graduated while she was still a sophomore.

Social life has shrunk to near zero. She can't just pick

up and go out for a pizza on two minutes' notice; she has to get a baby-sitter. Dating is almost nonexistent. Many guys aren't interested in a date who has a child. She's afraid to form a close relationship with a guy and have her son become attached to him. "If we'd break up, he'd lose someone too," she says.

Money is incredibly tight. She works 20 hours a week in addition to going to school; almost all of her income goes for things for her son, not for her.

The child's father lives far away and isn't very involved with his son, so Jenny tries to be both father and mother. Yet, as hard as it is, Jenny truly loves her little boy. She calls him "the greatest thing in my life." She'd be enjoying the experience much more, however, if it were after college and she was part of a parenting partnership.

If you get pregnant while you are at college, you don't have any good choices, says Linda McClintock, a psychotherapist with a Christian counseling agency. "For a Christian woman abortion is not an option," she says. "Yet, if you are pregnant, you will get a lot of pressure from friends and dorm mates who see it as the best choice."

They may not be around later if you regret that decision. Many women who have had abortions feel very guilty; a few become clinically depressed. Some have dropped out of college, unable to cope with their feelings or to accept God's message of forgiveness for any sin through the death of His Son.

There are also physical risks from abortion. The risk of miscarrying later pregnancies rises if you've had more than one abortion. Even with a "safe," sterile clinic abortion there is a risk of infection. Some otherwise healthy patients have even died from complications after abortion. There have been some studies that suggest that aborting a first pregnancy may raise your risk of breast cancer. (These studies are not conclusive proof at this time.)

The father of an aborted baby may seem to get off easily, but guys can also suffer guilt. Many of them deny it and bury their feelings deep inside.

A second option for an unplanned pregnancy is to give the baby up for adoption. "That's often the best choice for the child," says McClintock. "Two Christian parents making a home may be better for the child than being raised by a single parent." But, she points out, giving up a child for adoption involves deep pain. You bond to a child you carry in your body for nine months; you may need counseling to get through it.

Jenny's story shows that keeping the baby is not easy either. Raising a child is a big job, even for mature adults who are in a committed marriage. Going it alone is just about the hardest thing anyone can do.

Be aware that if you are a guy, you can't just walk away while the woman carries the burden. The courts will award and enforce child support payments, taking it directly from your paychecks, until the child is 18.

Here are a few facts about sex and pregnancy both men and women should know:

- It's possible for any act of intercourse to result in pregnancy. It can happen at any time of the month, it can happen the first time you have sex, it can happen whatever position or form of birth control you use. The only sure prevention is abstinence.

- It's rare, but a woman can become pregnant without penetration if the male ejaculates near the opening of the vagina.

- Sperm live in preejaculatory fluid, so even withdrawal before ejaculation (a method many heat-of-the-moment students depend on) can result in pregnancy.

- Sperm can live within a woman's body for 72 hours; the egg can live one to two days. Even if the woman ovulates a day or two after intercourse, pregnancy can still result. A woman's fertile time is usually around ovulation in the middle of her cycle, but so many factors can influence the cycle that you can't depend on it.

Debra Schaeffer Grime, M.D., is a Christian obstetrician/gynecologist. She's dealt with a lot of college-age women as well as young teens. She says she's seeing more sexually active college women than she did in the past. That's not a trend she thinks is a good thing, mainly because she's often called on to take care of the consequences.

Sexually transmitted diseases (STDs) are exploding on college campuses and, she says, students are often ignorant of the profound consequences that can come from infection with one of these bugs.

Some things you should know:

- 20 different infections—or more—can be transmitted during sex. A few, such as AIDS, can also be spread in other ways.

- Some STDs are caused by bacteria and can be cured with the proverbial shot of an antibiotic. Others come from viruses and can't be cured; the best you can hope for is control of their symptoms.

- Nobody ever said life is fair. STDs aren't fun for men, but for women they are even more serious. Women can pick them up much more easily, perhaps because of the fragile nature of vaginal tissue, but women also suffer much more serious aftereffects if they don't get treatment. Pelvic inflammatory disease

(PID) is a raging abdominal infection which often spreads to the uterus, fallopian tubes, ovaries, or other abdominal organs and can cause scar tissue to form. If your tubes become blocked with scar tissue, you might never be able to have a baby.

The most common STDs you as a college student should be aware of are

- *Chlamydia.* This nasty bug is the most common STD. You can get it only through intercourse and its primary site is the uterus, tubes, and ovaries. Caused by a bacteria, a woman can get it from a man and carry it in her system for months, never knowing it. Even if you are only infected once, you run a 25 percent risk of infertility, a second infection ups that to 50 percent. When symptoms are present (often there are none), they include vaginal or penile discharge, burning on urination, and mild pain just above the pubic bone. Chlamydia often results in PID. Oral sex with an infected person can lead to a throat inflammation. Chlamydia is treated with antibiotics; your sexual partner must be treated also.

- *Trichomoniasis.* You can have this one for a long time. It often produces no symptoms, especially in men but, when present, symptoms include a yellowish, foul-smelling discharge, genital irritation and itching, burning pain on urination. Trich can cause premature labor in a pregnant woman. It's treated with oral or vaginal antibiotics.

- *Gonorrhea.* This one's caused by a pus-producing bacteria; symptoms include a pus-filled discharge and itching or burning on urination. Gonorrhea is very easily transmitted; one act of intercourse with an infected person carries a 40 percent risk of developing the disease. In women it often leads to PID or infection in the Bartholin glands near the vaginal opening, causing them to become abscessed, a very painful condition. Males can carry the infection for a long time with no symptoms however, it can lead to strictures in the penis requiring painful dilation with small tubes. Gonorrhea is usually cured with antibiotics, but some strains are becoming resistant and harder to cure.

- *Human Papilloma Virus (HPV).* Does the thought of soft warts growing on your genitals make your skin crawl? Then you don't want this one! The warts can appear in both men and women, either internally or externally. They usually aren't uncomfortable; women especially may not even be aware of them. They are believed to cause abnormal cervical cells in many women, and in some, to lead to cervical cancer. There is no cure since the cause is a virus, but the warts themselves can be burned off with a laser or acid, or frozen off. If they become precancerous and have to be cut out, the cervix (the entrance to the uterus) may weaken enough to raise the risk of premature delivery in pregnancy.

- *Genital Herpes.* Caused by a virus, herpes produces blisters and sores in the genital and anal areas. They are very painful, beginning with a tingling or burning sensation. A first outbreak can be so painful the person cannot urinate. Herpes is spread by direct contact, either intercourse or oral-genital sex. Subsequent outbreaks are likely to be less severe than the first one, but they can occur months or even years later. The virus does not respond to antibiotics, so the infection cannot be cured. Symptoms can be suppressed with an expensive drug called acyclovir, but if infected, you have to learn to manage it and live with it. Fortunately, while painful and unpleasant, herpes doesn't cause serious consequences in the body, although there seems to be an increased risk of miscarriage or premature delivery if a woman is infected.

- *Syphilis.* This is often thought of as a disease of days gone by. Not so, it's a disease on the way back. Caused by an organism called a spirochete, the first sign of infection is a painless sore on the genitals. It goes away, but the infection has merely gone underground. In females the sore may be inside the body, virtually unnoticed; men are more often aware since the sore is on the outside. Fever, sore throat, and a rash may come next. In later stages, the disease causes severe neurological damage, blindness, dementia, and death. It can be cured with penicillin, but the drug is becoming less effective as resistant strains develop.

- *Hepatitis B.* About half of people with this STD don't show any symptoms; others have fever, head and muscle aches, fatigue, nausea, and yellowing of the eyes and skin. Hepatitis is caused by a virus. Most cases clear up without serious consequences, but some people become chronic carriers which increases risk for liver cancer.

- *HIV/AIDS.* You may think of AIDS as a disease that only homosexuals and drug users get. You may believe yourself safe if you are not in one of those two categories. However, the frightening truth is that AIDS is increasing in college students, spread through heterosexual sex. If infected, you can live for many years without symptoms, but once full-blown AIDS develops, it wreaks havoc on the immune system, allowing other infections to run rampant. Despite some new drugs that increase life span, there is no cure for AIDS. It is also transmitted through sharing needles used for injectable drugs, and passed from mother to child before birth. It's *not* spread by casual contact; you can't catch it even by living with an infected roommate.

If you'd like more information on sexually transmitted diseases, a good book is *Sexuality and Sexually Transmitted Diseases* by Joe S. McIlhaney, Jr. M.D. (Baker Book House, 1990).

We talked in a previous chapter about the pressure on college students to become sexually active and how to handle it. The facts about pregnancy and STDs should reinforce your resolve. Remember, by accepting God's plan for sex in our lives—sex only within the warmth of a committed, married relationship—you will protect yourself from all the terrible consequences that sexual promiscuity brings.

Dr. Schaeffer feels that communicating with the person you are dating about your sexual beliefs before you are in the heat of the moment is important. "So many young women have said to me, 'We never talked about sex until way into the relationship when I realized that he really wanted it. I didn't, but by then I really loved him, so I thought I should.'

"It's one of the things you should be talking about by the second or third date," she emphasizes, "the person's faith, what they believe in, who they are."

She points out that under God's law, sex outside of marriage is a sin. "There are always consequences for every sin," she says. "This one is no different from any other—it's forgiven through the death of Christ. But the consequences can still last a lifetime."

Campus Crime

Nobody likes to think about going off to college and being robbed. Or assaulted. Or raped. Yet it happens, more often than we might think—one research study done by the Campus Violence Prevention Center at Towson State College showed that one of three college students will be a crime victim.

For years it was hard to find out just how dangerous life on a particular campus might be, but the Crime Awareness and Campus Security Act of 1990 which took effect with the 1992 school year made it easier. That law requires any college accepting federal financial aid (and that's most of them!) to publish figures on all campus murders, rapes, robberies, and assaults during the previous three years and describe their campus security programs. You can usually get a copy of a campus crime pamphlet from the admissions department.

A serious look at violence on college campuses revealed two important facts: First, while some crimes are committed by outsiders, the majority (about 80 percent according to the Towson State study) are done by students. Second, the majority of perpetrators have been drinking. There's that same litany again: Alcohol fuels violence.

Most campuses, especially those in urban areas, have done a lot to increase security. The days of the open dorm where anyone could wander in are long gone. Dorms are now locked, rooms are often equipped with electronic locks, lighting has been increased, security patrols walk the campus, escort services will walk you to your car or dorm, phones have been installed along paths and in parking lots.

All of that helps, but you still have a responsibility to

help protect yourself. Here are some tips:

- Shed that "it can't happen to me" attitude. It can.
- Don't take expensive jewelry to college. Don't keep more than a few dollars in your room.
- *Use* the security systems that are in place. It may sound elementary, but always lock your door—too many students don't take the time when they are just running to the mailbox. Don't prop open outside doors so they won't lock; don't hold the door open for someone to enter if you don't know who he or she is. If you see someone in the dorm that you don't think should be there, report it. The Towson State study showed that after a crime incident on campus, students increased their security-conscious behavior for about two weeks, then reverted to normal.
- Don't walk alone at night. Go with a friend, or call the escort service. Avoid shadowed paths, dark parking lots, or empty buildings. That's all common sense, but common sense is your best friend on campus.

The stuff in this chapter isn't meant to scare you. Well, yes it is—a little! Too many students head off to college and come back a few months later shell-shocked by something terrible that happened to them. Sometimes they never return to college. And the sad thing is that many of those terrible occurrences—a drunken accident, a tragic result from a sexual encounter, being victim of a campus crime—could have been prevented. By knowing the risks before you go to college, you will have a much better chance of avoiding them. As the Holy Spirit works in your life, strengthening your relationship with Jesus through Bible study, regular worship, prayer, and fellowship with other Christians, you will be prepared to meet the challenges of college head on.

5

College Academics— It's Not High School Anymore

Mike was a good student in high school. He breezed through with a 3.9 GPA and cleaned up on the SAT. He went off to college expecting it to be a "little bit" harder—it turned out to be much more than a little bit. "College was a lot more work than I expected," he says reflectively. "I got flying A's in a couple of things I liked and was willing to spend some time on, but I didn't spend any time on my other classes."

Then there was his biggest distraction—work. "I got some money and then it was easier to work and get paid—and to justify it because I was being paid—than to sit behind the books," he says. Social life and partying, which trip up a lot of new college students, weren't a problem for him, but his ambition was. "I showed aptitude on the job, and there was an immediate reward, both in money and promotions; I was on the upward track."

Unfortunately, the upward track at work doesn't always blend well with the upward track at school. Mike finally "stopped out" (when you stop taking classes but don't formally drop out) while he worked full time for a while and spent some time clarifying what he was doing and where he was going.

Mike's story isn't unusual according to Jolene Hansen, who works with students in the Learning Lab at a University of Wisconsin Center. She's seen a lot of students who started their first college semester expecting to breeze through like they did in high school but were horrified when that first paper or first exam came back. "I've heard them say, 'A C! I never got a C in my life!'" she chuckles. "It can be a real shock."

This isn't high school. College is very different, and it can require a completely different set of habits and study skills. First, there's no one reminding you to get your work done—many kids hated having Mom prod them, but they discover in college how hard it is to function without that nudge. Second, professors in college don't care if you can spit back a bunch of facts on a test or in a paper; they are looking for a much deeper level of understanding and thought process.

Common Traps Freshmen Fall Into

To avoid the "reeling from first grades" syndrome that hits so many students about six weeks into their first semester, says Hansen, be aware of some pitfalls:

- **Overconfidence in your high school performance.** Some high schools are challenging and make their students work for grades, but many do not. "You may have gotten away with not studying in high school, but in college that won't work," she says. It's to your advantage to take the hardest courses you can find in high school, especially your senior year. Too many seniors save the easiest for last and lose their edge just before they really need it.

- **Not recognizing the depth of study that's necessary in college and how different from high school college is.** "It's no longer just memorizing facts," Hansen says. "You have to do in-depth thinking, the kind of thinking that comes from digging, reflecting, taking things apart, looking at the pieces, putting them back together, and coming up with your own conclusions." Sometimes that's called critical thinking. But whatever you label it, you'll need it—instead of just giving a conclusion, you'll have to show your thought process and how you arrived at your conclusion in both papers and essay exams. That type of thinking and studying may be very different from what you've been expected to do before. It takes more time, it takes more energy, but, says Hansen, it's also more satisfying. "When you don't do it, you are not truly becoming educated," she says.

- **Being unwilling to struggle to overcome a challenge.** Too many students get a C or a D on the first paper or test and conclude there's something wrong with the teacher, the test, or the course. Or, they decide they aren't cut out for college. An obstacle can become a step to learning if you use it that way, Hansen says. "That first low grade doesn't mean you're going to flunk out of college; it's a wake-up call," she says. "View it as a hurdle to climb over and learn in the process. You can come out on the other side more independent and responsible."

- **Lack of self-discipline.** Students often socialize too much, party too much—they haven't disciplined themselves to get the work done. In the past they may have depended on teachers to set deadlines, parents to prod them, friends to remind them. Now, in college, there are a lot of distractions: parties, sports events, endless "bull sessions," homesickness, falling in love, building a new social world. "They can all become excuses," Hansen says. "If you leave college work until the last minute, it doesn't get done very well. Procrastination does students in."

- **Not going to class.** That's an easy habit to fall into when no one is taking attendance. With a large lecture class it may seem as if no one cares whether you are there. You can always borrow notes from a friend and read the book. Beware of falling into that trap. In most classes there's much more than what shows up on paper—little hints, perceptions, ways of thinking—that aren't going to come through in borrowed notes. "Not going to class is the most foolish thing you can do!" Hansen emphasizes.

- **Working too much.** As Mike's experience shows, working can be a major obstacle to learning. Yes, college costs a lot, and no one wants to come out staggering under a load of debt. Most college students, both commuters and campus residents, have to work at least some. But know how much you can handle. Keep your priorities in order—school has to come first. It won't do you any good to be debt-free if you wash out!

- **Not recognizing the signs of trouble early enough.** Letting friends make your decisions about when to study and when to socialize, going home too often as a way to escape pressure, not sleeping enough, or, conversely, sleeping too much as a way of hiding, using alcohol to avoid facing work, skipping class because you haven't done the reading, finding justification for not doing the reading—"I wouldn't have gotten anything out of it anyway," blaming the professor—"Nobody could learn anything from her." Does that litany sound familiar? If so, face the facts—trouble may be looming on the horizon.

Keeping Out of Trouble

The best way to handle academic trouble is to prevent it in the first place, says Janet Brown, Ph.D., director of the Study Center at the University of Wisconsin, Waukesha. Good study skills can make all the difference. Whole books have been written on how to study in college—we can't go into the subject in any kind of depth in just one chapter, but Dr. Brown can offer you a few tips.

- **Get a good book on study skills before you go to college.** Even if you think you know how to study, a book can sharpen your skills and give you an edge. There's a list of good study skills books at the end of this chapter.

- **Get organized.** You'll need a day planner. You can spend big bucks for a Filofax and feel like a professional, or you can do it with an 89 cent notebook. Or, you can use the organizer or calendar feature on a laptop computer. But have one place in which to record all the deadlines for all your classes. Many experts recommend a three-ring binder for all your class notes and hand-outs rather than separate notebooks. That way everything is with you all the time, and you can use odd moments that otherwise would be wasted because the right notebook is back in the dorm. Speaking of wasting odd moments, many students are amazed to learn that there are 168 hours in every week—it wakes them up to think how many hours can be frittered away in front of the TV or hanging out.

- **Accept college experts' study-time recommendations.** It may be a bit of a shock, but most experts say you should be prepared to spend two to three hours per week studying for each credit hour the course carries—in addition to the hours you spend in class. That means a three credit course will require 6–9 hours of study time each week. A four credit course will burn up 8–12 hours. Multiply that by the number of courses you plan to carry and you will get an idea of your "work week." Treat college like a 40-hour-a-week job. It will be, and then some.

- **Learn how to go to class.** First, go. Every time. Sit in the front—the back row is for people who want to sleep. "Students often go to a lecture like they are going to hear a story," says Dr. Brown. "But college requires a different kind of listening." Pay strict attention. Active listeners learn more than passive listeners. You also need to prepare for each lecture by doing the reading—you won't get nearly as much out of it if you go in cold. And you need to take the time right after the lecture to go over your notes, fill in any blanks, and make sure you can summarize what you just heard.

  Some students tape-record lectures. That helps some people, but it takes a great deal of time if you listen to each lecture a second time. Dr. Brown suggests you use the tapes of the first few lectures to compare with your notes; once you are sure you are getting everything down you can discontinue taping. By the way, ask first—some professors don't like to be taped. If the professor says no to taping, ask him or her to review your notes with you to make sure you're getting it all. Most professors will appreciate the effort you're making.

- **Learn to take good notes.** There are a couple of effective systems. Many people use an outline/key word approach in which they make a formal outline of what they are hearing. That, of course, works best when a professor is organized; you may have to rewrite notes from a disorganized lecture. The Cornell method divides a page into three sections: a 2½" left margin in which you write questions and key words about what you are learning, a main body in which you actually record the facts from the lecture, and a 2" strip across the bottom in which you write a summary of what's on that page. "Clustering" or "mind mapping" is a visual form of notetaking in which you write a key point in a circle and then draw arrows from the main circle to smaller circles for the supporting points. These methods are explained in detail in most study skills books. Experiment to find the one that works best for you.

  Many students bring a laptop computer to college and use it to take notes—some even started that practice in high school. If you choose to take your notes that way, make sure you have a folder or three-ring binder with you to store handouts. If you're using a laptop, it's still important to keep your notes organized. Set up a different folder for each class. Decide if you want to make each class session a different document or one continuous document. If you choose to use one of the notetaking methods discussed above, set up a template for yourself so you're not formatting a document as you take notes. Just as you would if you were writing on paper, go over your notes after class. (It can actually be easier to rearrange your notes on a laptop than on paper.) It may seem like common sense, but make sure you either have a place to plug your laptop in during class or that your battery has enough power to last through the lecture. Also, don't forget to make a daily backup of your files. A corrupt file could be disastrous. Again, the important thing is to find the methods of notetaking and studying that work for you and *use them*.

- **Learn to read a textbook effectively.** Most texts, Dr. Brown says, give students a lot of helping devices, but few students use them. "Probably only one in 1,000 students reads the preface to a textbook," she says, "but it explains how the book is set up to help you study." Most chapters have study guides in the beginning and review helps at the end, but again, most students skip them and plunge into the text.

   Most people need to highlight passages or take some sort of notes to really understand a textbook since many textbooks are densely packed with ideas and information. How you synthesize the information is up to you, but when you are finished with a chapter, you should be able to state the overall theme and have a way to organize and recall the details. You may have been taught the SQ3R system in high school—it's a pretty common method. SQ3R stands for **Survey** (read the subheadings in the chapter and the summary); **Question** (turn each subheading into a question that you will answer by reading the section); **Read**, **Recite** (read the text, then look away from the book and recite the answer to your questions); **Review** (when you've finished reading all the sections, go back and review the major points and subpoints).

   A word about highlighting: Don't do it as you

read, you'll highlight everything. Go back and highlight after you're done reading; then it will also serve as a review. Some students outline a textbook, or type two- or three-page summaries of each chapter. Again, a good book on study skills will give you much more information about how to read a textbook. Ultimately, you need to decide which method works best for *you*.

• **Learn to study effectively for tests.** Some profs give you the course in their lectures, others expect you to get the basics from the text while they use their lectures to amplify and give examples. Know which kind of prof you've got. If he's a lecture-lover, study mainly from your notes and use the text as a supplement. If she sees the text as primary, study mainly from the book. How do you know? Ask. "It's perfectly reasonable to ask a professor before the first test if the exam will be mainly on the book or the lectures," says Dr. Brown. "Freshman often think you can't ask those questions, but you can."

Then use every technique you can to master the material. The most efficient way to learn is to file bits of information in short-term memory, then dredge them up a bunch of times, organizing them, analyzing them, saying them over and over. That lets your brain establish pathways. Constant review is your best friend. So, memorize vocabulary and sample problems, be sure you can thoroughly outline each chapter, have terms down cold. Use flash cards, outlines tacked to the wall, summary sheets, mnemonics (e.g., In 1492 Columbus sailed the ocean blue), acronyms (e.g., ROY G BIV for the colors of the rainbow), keywords, or whatever works for you. That ever-handy study skills book can offer a host of additional hints.

Many studies have shown that you get the most out

of a study session during the first hour; after that your learning curve plunges. Study your hardest subject first, take a break after an hour, consider switching to another subject for the next hour, and then come back to the first.

- **Get yourself into a study group.** You can study by yourself, or you can study with others; most people find a study group an enormous help. Structure it so the group doesn't descend to a general rehash of material you already know. Assign different people to thoroughly learn different parts of the material and explain it to the others. One good technique is to have each person prepare a couple of questions as if for an exam. Everyone in the group tries answering them, then the person who wrote them explains.

- **Practice good test-taking skills.** Get there early and use the time to calm your mind—a bit of prayer never hurts! Once the test has begun, jot sample problems you've memorized or key ideas you need to cover in an essay on the back of the test to relieve memory pressure. Use all of the time—just because someone else finishes early doesn't mean you should too. Make sure you read every word of the directions and every word of the questions—don't get stuck writing all the essays because you didn't notice the instructions said to choose two! Do the easy parts first to get rolling; they may provide a review for the harder parts. But leave enough time do to the hard parts. Remember, you should allow 60 percent of your time for a 60-point question (on a 100-point scale). Again, check your study skills book and find a system that works for you.

When you get a test back, analyze your mistakes. Did you study the wrong things? How much of the test came from the book, how much from the lectures? Where can you find the correct answers to questions you missed? Make notes on the test on how to do better on the next one. If the professor won't let you keep the test, make notes in your notebook to prepare for the next test.

When Grades Go South

Suppose you've done all this stuff and you're still in trouble. Then what?

Jolene Hansen has some suggestions:

- **Plan your time better.** Perhaps you need to make a formal schedule for each week, listing the hours you spend in class and slotting in study time. Then stick to it. Sounds too regimented, you say? If you're having trouble getting all your work done, it may be the only answer.

- **Assess your individual learning style and try to accommodate it.** Many study skills books have quizzes you can take to see if you are an auditory or visual learner. Know yourself and what you need. If you're visually oriented, use graphs and charts to master the work; if you learn better through hearing, tape lectures or read texts aloud to yourself.

- **Ask for help.** Most colleges have learning centers and tutoring available for the asking. It's not a sign of failure to use these resources. Quite the opposite— it's often the best students you see there. "The ones who are failing are back in the dorm playing cards," Hansen quips. Ask your professor for help. He or she is not going to become your tutor but may be able to offer suggestions on what to concentrate on or how to study better for the class. In college that's not considered "brown nosing" like it was in high school. There are some profs who are unapproachable and won't take the time to help, but the majority like students who are interested and make an effort and will go the extra mile.

- **Take responsibility for your own learning.** Don't make excuses. Maybe your roommate does keep you up half the night, maybe the prof is hard to understand, maybe the amount of reading is overwhelming—even if all those are true, they still aren't excuses. Find ways to cope with them.

- **If you are overwhelmed, consider lightening your load.** Some students can carry 16 credits a semester. Some start to sink when they go over 12 or 13. It's to your advantage to do better in fewer classes—would you rather have 16 credits with a 2.0 average, or 12 with a 3.0? Sometimes getting out in four years isn't possible.

- **Keep a learning journal.** When you finish a project, paper, or test, reflect on it in writing. How could you have done better? What would have made it easier? What lessons did you learn? What did you do well? Be very honest. Those reflections can keep you on track and head off problems.

Mike, by the way, is back in college. He progressed with his company to the point where they are willing to pay his tuition and give him flexible hours so he can better combine work and school. That may not be the best solution for everyone, but it's working for him.

Asked what advice he would give to people just starting college, the word "goals" jumped from his mouth. "If you don't have a plan for what you want from your life and how the next few years are going to contribute to that, you need to start thinking about those things," he says. "Start with long-term goals and then break them down into smaller achievable tasks. You have to take that process right down to the daily level—plan your time to meet your immediate goal: passing the classes you have right now." That, he says, is the only way to reach the long-range goal: a diploma on your wall.

If all of these study tips have you thinking, "I need to study about how to study?!" relax. The important thing is that you *learn* what your professors are teaching. Try one or two of the methods suggested. If they aren't working, try another. Talk to friends and find out how they study. Ultimately, it's the learning that's important, not the procedure you used to get there.

A Word about Cheating

Cheating seems to be pervasive on college campuses. Two researchers, Donald McCabe and Linda Klebe Trevino, surveyed over 6,000 students at 31 college campuses around the country in 1993, asking questions about cheating. Two thirds of their subjects admitted to cheating at least once—even while 80 percent agreed with the statement that cheating was never justified under any circumstances.

Cheating behaviors included copying from another person's test, using crib notes, plagiarizing material on papers, falsifying a bibliography on a paper, turning in work that was done by someone else, and working together on assignments that require individual work.

They also found that students believe that very few cheaters are ever caught, and they say that the attitude of their peers is the determining factor in whether they cheat. On campuses where honor codes were in effect, there was less cheating; on campuses where people who cheat were looked down on, there was less cheating.

As a Christian student, you don't need an honor

code to tell you not to cheat. We have a code we carry around with us all the time—the Ten Commandments. God's people, living in response to His love, will take their responsibility to be honest seriously. Even when the temptation to take the easy way out is overpowering, Christian students can turn to God and ask for the strength to resist temptation.

But even more than not cheating yourself, this survey shows the effect Christian students can have on the society in which we live. Speak out about your Christian values; let your fellow students know that you think it's unethical to cheat. Make it clear that you won't cheat and that you think it's wrong of others to do so. McCabe and Trevino found that the most important determiner of student cheating is the climate or culture of academic integrity on a campus. Be part of that culture—help make it happen.

A Few Good Study Guides

College Is Only the Beginning: A Student Guide to Higher Education by John N. Gardner and A. Jerome Jewler. Wadsworth Publishing, 1989.

Becoming a Master Student by David B. Ellis. Houghton Mifflin, 1994.

The Confident Student by Carol C. Kanar. Houghton Mifflin, 1991.

How to Study in College by Walter Pauk. Houghton Mifflin, 1988.

Studying Smart by Diana S. Hunt and Pam Hait. Harper Collins, 1990.

Manage Your Time by Ron Fry. Career Press, 1994.

6

NURTURING YOUR FAITH ON A SECULAR CAMPUS

"After having gone to Lutheran schools all my life, I was looking forward to the challenge of being in a secular college," says Brad, looking back at his college experience. "But I knew what I was in for, and I don't think a lot of kids do. I went into it knowing that I needed to get connected with other Christians on campus right from the start. We all need the fellowship of other believers just to balance the crud we get hit with in the world—there's safety in numbers! That's even more true on a secular campus where there are so many people hostile to the faith and so many temptations and readily-available sources of sin."

Unfortunately, says Rev. John Pless, campus pastor at the University of Minnesota, a lot of new college students don't realize that, and they don't seek out Christian friendship and support. "I see a lot of kids coming on campus, even ones from Christian homes, who just don't go to church at all," he says.

Why do so many kids let their faith lapse during college, despite the very real risk that once lapsed it may never revive? There are several reasons:

- **Peer pressure.** "The statistics I read say that 90 percent of our campus is unchurched," says Rev. Pless. "I like the Phillips' paraphrase of a passage in Romans 12 where Paul says, 'Don't let the world around you squeeze you into its own mould' " [J. B. Phillips, *The New Testament in Modern English*, Macmillan Publishers, 1972]. I think that happens on a university campus where students are confronted with professors who dismiss Christianity as primitive myth, with a world view of toleration of every kind of lifestyle, with a culture that defines itself without any reference to God."

  He's not saying, he points out, that students who come to college as Christians become atheists, rather that they stop actively living their faith.

- **Freedom to choose not to go to church.** When you lived at home and the family was going to church, you were strongly urged, maybe even required to go along. Now you're on your own; Mom's not waking you on Sunday morning anymore. "It's your first taste of freedom and not going to church is an easy way to rebel," says Drew, also a recent graduate who saw his faith grow during his years on a secular campus.

- **Time pressure and stress.** College is stressful and the demands on your time are great. It can be very easy to sleep in on Sunday morning or to skip Bible study because you've got too much other studying to do. But remember that one of the antidotes to stress is quieting your mind and focusing on something other than schoolwork. Quiet time with God, whether at church or in private devotion, can give you that stress relief. When your mind is quiet and open to God's power, He can use that time to take away your stress and fill you with His blessings.

How do you counteract the temptation to let your faith slide while you are at college? By actively choosing to get involved in some type of campus religious life. The opportunity is certainly there.

Finding Support for Your Faith

"There are two things you need for your spiritual life in college," says Brad. "One is a good, solid church for worship, the other is a group of other Christian students to be in fellowship with. At some universities you can get both in one place, in others you can't."

He points out that a lot of churches in university towns have active student groups. There are also many Christian ministries, some sponsored by denominations and others that are interdenominational, on most every campus. "In my opinion it's good to be involved in a group that's on your campus in addition to a church," Brad says, "because it gives you an opportunity to get involved with outreach and witnessing your faith on campus. That evangelism training is something you will carry with you for the rest of your life."

Drew's story probably illustrates a common pattern. His small, state university didn't have a full-time campus ministry for his denomination. He tried the Protestant service at the Ecumenical Center a few times but, he says, it didn't inspire him to come back. "I didn't really look for anything else at first," he recalls. "I just floated. When I went home for the weekend, I'd go to church, but when I was at school I didn't even think about it." It wasn't until a friend invited him to a campus Bible study that he started hearing about some of the churches in town. One Lutheran church, he found out, actually sent a bus to the dorms on Sunday morning to pick up students. He decided to give it a try and spent the next five years actively involved in that church.

There are similar choices at every college:

- Some big universities have a full-time campus pastor with the equivalent of a congregation right on campus. Other, smaller colleges may have a part-time ministry or just an outreach that provides students with a way to get to a church in town.

- Even if your campus doesn't have a full-time pastor for your denomination, there may be a campus chapter of a national Christian or denominational students' group. Besides local Bible studies, social events, and a chance to form close, supportive Christian friendships, study groups also sponsor regional retreats, workshops, and national gatherings. Even if there's no chapter on your campus, you can join a national group, get their mailings, and attend the gatherings. Some can also provide you with excellent materials for personal Bible study. You might consider starting a group on your campus if there isn't one.

- Rev. Pless cautions that some groups are often very liberal and activist on social issues such as abortion and homosexuality. If you're interested in a group, find out what they believe and practice. If you aren't comfortable with their views, find a different group.

- Look into national interdenominational student groups such as Campus Crusade for Christ, Navigators, and Intervarsity Christian Fellowship. Again, go in prepared—if you aren't comfortable with their doctrines, go somewhere else.

- There are also small local groups not affiliated with any national group often called "para-church" organizations. "I see many more of these on campus now, as some of the national groups are declining in membership," Rev. Pless says. "They have names such as Great Commission Fellowship, Christian Fellowship, or Campus Fellowship. Many of them are just informal groups of students who get together for friendship or Bible study."

You need to look at each one individually, he says. Some of them are the campus outreach of a local church in the community, and that's fine as long as they are truthful about who sponsors them. Some advertise themselves as nondenominational but are actually sponsored by a single church body. "It's a matter of truth in advertising," he says.

These national and local groups have their pros and cons according to Rev. Pless:

The pluses:

- They can provide a source of support and Christian fellowship, especially if there is no group for your particular denomination. They can be a place to meet other Christians and to make friends with people who aren't into the sex and excessive drinking scene. Spending Saturday night at a Christian fellowship barbecue can be a better option than spending it hitting the bars.

- They sometimes provide a "first contact" for non-Christian students, a first chance to hear the Gospel message. They may give you a framework in which to witness your faith to the non-Christian students around you.

- They can help you see how God is present right on your campus. "People share a lot about how God is working in their lives in campus groups," says Drew. "That made me think about how God was working in my life also; it was inspiring."

- They urge personal devotion and Bible study and can give you tools and methods to do that.

- They may give you the push you need to get to church. "My group really encouraged us to find a church of our own faith in town," says Drew.

The minuses:

- They don't always teach clear, biblical doctrine. Some tend to be millennial, teaching a literal belief that Christ will reign for a thousand years on earth before the world ends. Many of them also discount infant baptism and place little importance on the Lord's Supper (although, in fairness, providing the sacraments isn't really their "job").

- Some base the way of salvation on a decision to accept Christ. The Bible teaches us that we don't make a decision but that the Holy Spirit has chosen us.

- Some tend to base belief more on emotion than knowledge. "Many students find an emotional awakening of their faith in these groups but then find that emotion can take them only so far," Rev. Pless says. "When they start reading the Scripture, they come on questions they need answers for." Some groups offer real Bible studies that provide intellectual knowledge; some don't.

If you choose to attend any of these national or local para-church groups, go in with your eyes open. Take advantage of the chance for friendship and Christian fun they offer, but be aware of some of their differences in doctrine. And don't ever substitute them for worship and sacraments in a real church.

"You need the balance of being in a church," Brad emphasizes. "Outreach is not worship, and worship is not necessarily outreach, but both are an integral part of Christian life. So a campus ministry group, whether denominational or interdenominational, is not a substitute for a church. There may be no sacraments, and the group is likely to be too small and select. You need to be in a church that's a cross section of the body of Christ."

What will happen to your faith while you are at college? It's largely up to you. God will always be there for you and the Holy Spirit will continue working in you. But you have to choose to nurture your faith, to put yourself in situations where it can grow. "Go back to John 15 where it says, 'I am the vine; and you are the branches'," says Rev. Pless. "Stay connected with the Vine. You do that through worship, through God's Word, and through receiving the Lord's Supper."

"You are about to grow in college in more ways than you've ever grown before, intellectually and socially," Brad says. "And you have the opportunity to grow spiritually as well, even at a secular university. The college years are the most formative years of your life. They are the time when most people either make the transition from a passive, childlike faith to an active, vibrant, adult faith—or their faith just dies. It's easy for that to happen in college, so it's critical that you seek out others who are in the same situation so you can grow in faith together."

A Few Words about Cults

Perhaps you don't remember the heyday of cults back in the late 1970s and early 1980s. The Moonies were accused of brainwashing college students; parents paid deprogrammers to forcefully remove their children from the group's clutches. Hare Krishnas danced in college quads in their saffron robes and with their shaved heads. Newspapers and magazines were filled with articles about people who had escaped cults and warnings to college students to avoid cults.

You don't hear as much about cults anymore. The Moonies seem to have gone mainstream, some of the other big cults dissolved when their leaders died or got embroiled in a scandal. But according to Jim Valentine of CARIS (Christian Apologetics and Research Information Service) which researches information on cults, they haven't gone away. "Some cult groups have become less prominent on college campuses than they were in the past, but other groups are taking their places," he says. "Many of the groups that are most active these days are more dangerous because they look much closer to Christianity than the Moonies or Krishnas did."

What exactly is a cult? Herbert F. Beck, in his book *How to Respond to the Cults*, defines a cult as "a group of people gathered about a specific person or person's interpretation of the Bible." He emphasizes that cults can come from any religion, not just Christianity. Black Muslims are a cultic deviation from the religion of Islam, and Hare Krishna is a form of Hinduism.

There are some characteristics that most cults share:

- They claim to be part of a major religion such as Christianity, but when you look at their central doctrines, especially around the nature of Christ and the way of salvation, they are not truly Christian.

- They use manipulation of guilt and fear to keep members. Often they teach that without the group you are doomed; the only way to salvation is through their leader's revelation. As Jim Valentine puts it, "They use Satan's native language—lies—to recruit and control people and teach others to use lies also."

- They often dwell on the end of the world, complete with dire warnings about the battles that are to come.

- They use a form of "double talk," using Christian words such as grace, salvation, or redemption but with entirely different meanings.

- They believe that "their way" will be proved right in the end and everyone else will be proved wrong.

- They control their members and require a highly disciplined way of life. Some allow very little contact with the outside world; others allow contact but require strict obedience.

Why are cults so dangerous? Because, Jim Valentine says, depending on what the cult teaches, if they lead you to believe something that denies the essence of Christianity, you may risk your eternal salvation. In addition, they can cause extreme estrangement in families and severe psychological damage. Many cult members have become convinced that they cannot function outside the cult; some have been driven to suicide. In 1997, the cult known as Heaven's Gate, led by Marshall Applegate, committed mass suicide. The members believed Applegate when he told them they needed to leave their earthly vehicles (their bodies) so they could all move to a higher level—a spaceship they believed was at the end of the Hale Bopp comet.

The deaths of the 39 cult members devastated their families. Two former Heaven's Gate members even attempted their own suicide several weeks after the group suicide. One of them was successful. The cult mentality has a very real grip on even the strongest will.

You don't have to go to a special place or hang out with certain types of people to get involved with a cult. Unsuspecting Internet surfers have stumbled across the websites of cults. Especially if the website is well-designed, it can lure you into the group. Once you've taken the bait, members can chat with you or e-mail you to keep you interested. All of this can seem very innocent. It can even be comforting to a college student who is homesick or lonely or searching for acceptance. But once a cult has its hooks in you—even across cyberspace—it's hard to get away.

So what other cults are out there? It's difficult to give a list of cults operating on college campuses today because they are so fluid, often changing their names. By the time you read this, half the cults mentioned could be gone and new ones could have taken their places.

But there are several that have been around for a while and seem to center on college campuses:

- **The International Church of Christ** which sometimes adds the name of the city in which it's located to its name (e.g., the Boston Church of Christ). They are not to be confused with the United Church of Christ, or the southern fundamentalist church called Church of Christ, or the Church of God in Christ—all legitimate church bodies.

- **University Bible Fellowship** which sounds mainstream but is very controlling and destructive of families.

117

- **The Local Church** (sometimes called Living Stream Ministries or Christians on Campus) which teaches that God was first the Father, then the Son, and is now the church and we are mingled with Him.

- **The Way International** nearly disappeared after the death of its founder, but it seems to be rebuilding. Eastern and New Age movements are on every campus, along with larger mainstream cultlike groups such as the Jehovah's Witnesses and the Mormons.

How do you know if a campus group is legitimate or a cult? Here is a list of red flag warnings from Jim Valentine:

- **Have you ever heard of them before?** If you haven't and you can't find information on them anywhere, be suspicious.

- **Do they say they have exclusive answers to questions of salvation?** If they teach that you can reach God only through them, watch out.

- **Do they flatter you too much, give you extreme attention?** In the days of the Moonies that was called "love bombing" and was used to break through a student's feeling of being alone and lonely.

- **Do they dominate your time?** A legitimate group will not ask you to give up studying, friends, and family so you can devote more time to them.

- **Do they put down your family?** Some groups encourage you not to talk to your parents, not to go home to visit, but to spend all your breaks and vacations with them. In extreme cases some groups have told members that their parents are the tools of Satan, working to keep them from the truth.

- **Do their doctrines sound extreme?** Many cults

118

revolve around a person. Do they tell you that their leader has special revelations, that you must follow him or her to be saved? The Bible tells us we have one mediator—Christ. If the leader becomes the mediator, that's a warning.

- **Do they dwell on the end times and the fulfillment of prophecy?** Beware, especially if their preoccupation with the end times involves fear or paints a scenario of horrible things to come.

If you think you've become involved with a cult, there are several things you should do.

First, talk to your campus pastor, your home pastor, your parents, the dean of students, or the leaders of real campus Christian organizations. Get all the information you can. You can call CARIS at 414-771-7379. They don't know about every single group in the country, but they know about many of them and know where to get information on the others.

If the members won't leave you alone even when you've told them you don't want to be part of the group, ask for help. Have friends intercept phone calls or knocks on the door. Stay away from the places where the group hangs out. Tell the dean, your RA, or the campus pastor; sometimes they can warn cult members away. If you choose to confront them, don't let them sit down with you and explain it all away—people can twist words very easily. "Don't listen, don't let them sweet talk you out of leaving," says Valentine.

Most important, stay alert. "God certainly wants to be in your life, but He doesn't want to make you a mindless puppet under the abusive leadership of another human being," Valentine says. "Don't check your brains at the door! Check things out with objective sources outside the cult. Remember, a cult leader's assurance that he is not a cult leader isn't enough."

So how *will* you nurture your faith in college? As Brad said at the beginning of this chapter, "We all need the fellowship of other believers just to balance the crud we get hit with in the world." That fellowship can be in the study of God's Word, in service to His people, in the sharing of the Lord's Supper, or in just hanging out with fellow Christians. Take time to do each of these things. You won't believe the difference it will make in your life—during college and for years to come.

7

WALKING A MINEFIELD

The College Political Scene

Tammy remembers her first class in Introduction to Sociology. The very first thing the professor said was, "I'm a feminist, a liberal Democrat, and a lesbian." Tammy wondered what the teacher's political and sexual preference had to do with sociology—it would, Tammy says, have taken her aback just as much had the professor announced that she was a conservative Republican heterosexual.

Things didn't get much better. At one point Tammy used the word *role* referring to the many aspects of women's lives: wife, mother, worker. "She really attacked me," Tammy says. "She shouted, 'What do you mean, *role*!' She constantly told us that women should be totally independent and even if they made the choice to marry and have children, they should never feel bound by those choices." When Tammy said she was a Christian, the professor's response was that we all have our views, but that Tammy would learn in college to change hers.

Welcome to the college political scene. Of course, it varies greatly from campus to campus. You may identify with the experiences of the students in this chapter when you get to college or you may think, "What are they talking about? It's not like that at all." It all depends on your particular school.

It's probably safe to say that the political atmosphere is more intense at big universities, especially on the east and west coasts. But there are plenty of exceptions—Tammy's experience was at a Midwestern community college and two of the other students referred to in this chapter went to small, private women's colleges.

The political atmosphere on a college campus is not limited to the differences between Democrats and Republicans. It encompasses issues that polarize people, placing them in radically opposed camps. You may run into a political atmosphere where the predominant attitude says there's only one acceptable way to view certain issues, only one viewpoint that can be expressed on such things as race, sexual preference, or abortion, and that conflicting views will not be tolerated or even discussed. Such a political atmosphere is the antithesis of what a college or university should be: a place where every idea can be expressed, discussed, and explored.

Just as the political atmosphere is more radical on some campuses than others, it is also more prevalent in certain departments, namely the humanities and social sciences. You may spend four years in college and never run into any pressure at all. Or, you may feel, as Christine (whom we'll meet later) did, that she was walking through a minefield every day and was challenged every time she opened her mouth.

There are a number of different political pressures you may face on campus; we'll look at three: the feminist world view, abortion, and the usually positive pressure to be sensitive to others.

The "Women's Studies" View of Life

Feminist. That word arouses a lot of feelings in people, feelings that range from pride and admiration to "not me!" The reason there are so many different reactions to that word is that there are so many different aspects of feminism. Describing someone as a *feminist* tells you almost nothing about what he or she believes.

Before we go any further, let's be very clear about something: God never intended women to be discriminated against. He gave women many abilities and as the illustration in Proverbs describes, He expects women to fully use those gifts. St. Paul says in Galatians 3:28, "There is neither Jew nor Greek, slave nor free, male nor female, for you are all one in Christ Jesus."

Let's also be clear about something else: Today's women owe a great debt to the feminists of the past. The early ones, the suffragettes, worked tirelessly to get women the right to vote and own property. Without them a woman wouldn't go to the polls on election day or be able to own that shiny new car in her own name. A later wave of feminists worked to get women equal access to higher education, work opportunities, and equal pay. Without them the young women who are reading this probably wouldn't be going to college and certainly wouldn't have the option to major in law, medicine, or engineering. So "feminism" is not necessarily a dirty word.

However, today there are many branches of feminism: Marxist feminism, psychological feminism, eco-feminism, and radical feminism, to name just a few. Some have gone far beyond working for equality and have adopted a world view that says women are victims of oppression and men are the oppressors. Some of them go so far as to advocate total separation from men—the enemy. For want of a better term, I will refer to them as radical feminists (sometimes in the press they are called militant feminists).

While they are a minority, they do have a strong presence and a great deal of power on some college campuses. They run many women's studies programs and influence other departments also, especially in the humanities and social sciences. You may take a whole string of women's studies and social science courses and never run into a feminist, or, every such course you take may be taught by a feminist.

What do radical feminists believe and teach? Dr. William Weinrich, professor of early church history at Concordia Theological Seminary in Ft. Wayne, Indiana, has done a study of the roots of feminism as part of his interest in church history. There are three core beliefs, he says, which underlie radical feminism:

1. **There are no differences between men and women.** All differences between the sexes are created by society for the purpose of keeping women in an inferior position.

2. **The world is fundamentally a hostile place.** This leads to a siege mentality, the feeling that everything in society is there to oppress you.

3. **There is no objective truth.** All statements of truth are politically constructed and are meant to maintain the power of the person making the statement. What is right or wrong for you therefore may not be for me.

As Christians, Dr. Weinrich says, we cannot accept any of these assertions. "The distinction between men and women is vital," he says. "It's part of God's creation. God is clear that men and women are created equal, but within that common humanity there is real difference."

He also points out that we do have real truth—given to us in God's revelation. And we do have objective standards of right and wrong. What God has said is wrong is not subject to our cultural interpretation.

Radical feminism is largely hostile to religions—not just Christianity, but also Judaism or Islam—because they teach that there is a God who has a higher will and calls us to live by certain values. "The idea that there is a higher will who can make claims on us is the essence of hierarchy and patriarchy and is therefore oppressive in their view," Dr. Weinrich says.

How do those views play out on the campus? The experiences of Christine and Rosalie are examples.

Christine started college right after high school, but since she got married after her second year, her situation was a bit different from the average student's. Rosalie was also a nontraditional student. She went to college as an adult. She was married and had several children. Both Christine and Rosalie attended small, private women's colleges.

"The underlying theme in the courses I took was that women have been oppressed throughout history and now it's time to declare our strength and superiority," Christine says. "I didn't have a problem with seeing myself as an educated woman with all the potential in the world to be whatever I want to be. I did have a problem with the viewpoint I heard expressed that men are not necessary in society except for procreation; that women can do it all themselves. I think it takes all of us to make life happen well, and I think men have a lot to offer."

Rosalie found the same theme in her college. "They negated all responsibility for men," she says. "Women, in their view, can do it all themselves. And should. Their viewpoint was that men have really bolixed everything up and therefore women should take over the power and not share it. I remember asking a professor, 'What do I tell my son? What is his responsibility?'" The answer, she felt, was that he had none.

A word that ran through Rosalie's courses was *deconstruction*. All society's institutions she explains—the church, the government, and especially the family—have to be deconstructed and reconstructed according to a feminist viewpoint. "That viewpoint is that all those institutions are oppressive," she says.

Another common theme was that all viewpoints are equal (unless, of course, the viewpoint was Christian) and that no one has a right to judge someone else's view. Christine found that theme especially in a course called Philosophy of Love and Friendship that she took to fulfill a philosophy requirement. "Most of the class readings were about homosexual relationships," she remembers. "But one was about bestiality [sex with an animal]. That was very offensive to me; I thought it was inappropriate and not necessary to understand someone's philosophy of love." She objected to the reading and was allowed to substitute a different one, but the professor told her that we all come from different walks of life and things are only morally unacceptable for some people. "The message was that there is no right and wrong, it's all culturally determined and I didn't have the right to judge someone else's actions," she says.

Both women felt they were viewed with suspicion both for being Christians and for having chosen marriage. "Married women were made to feel irrelevant," says Rosalie. "I remember one lecture in which the professor referred to women who chose to stay home with their children in such a disdainful fashion that I could hardly sit and listen. That option was always presented in a very negative way, with a lot of talk about independence from male dominance." It didn't matter that Rosalie favored equal education, opportunity, and pay. "You had to accept the whole thing or nothing," she says. "I was classified as 'pro-family' and that was a term of derision."

Christine found herself in a double bind. She was doing the "right" thing by going to college and preparing for a career, but she felt put down because her husband was supporting her while she did so. "I was supposed to be independent and do it myself," she says.

Christine was an education major. In one class she had to write a paper about her philosophy of life and how that would be reflected in her philosophy of education. "To be frank, my philosophy of life was wrong," she says. "It would have been unacceptable for me to say that I would model values for my students—you might influence them, and you don't have the right to do that." She wasn't talking about religious values she points out, just general values such as honesty and loyalty. "In my teachers' view there is no universal set of values. I had to create a philosophy that would please them because I needed to pass the course, so I just wrote about all children having an equal opportunity to education. It was very shallow and not at all me, but it was what they wanted to hear."

While neither Rosalie nor Christine was ever subjected to real rudeness in class, that has happened in some schools. Writer Dinesh D'Souza, in his book *Illiberal Education: the Politics of Race and Sex on Campus*, tells about a women's studies course at a college in Seattle in which the teacher told the class that the traditional American family is a dysfunctional family unit. When some students questioned this assertion, they were shouted down by a couple of teaching assistants who yelled "Denial, denial."

The *Wall Street Journal* reported on a survey of students at Wellesley, an east coast women's college, that said 30 percent of students in a women's studies program felt silenced or at risk of attack if they expressed an unpopular opinion. Said one, "There's usually a predominately feminist opinion in class, and it is difficult to go against this attitude."

By the way, while this issue mainly affects women, men aren't immune. Some men do take women's studies courses, and many take other courses in the humanities and social sciences where these viewpoints reign. Sometimes the feminist classroom can be an uncomfortable place for a man; in other classrooms male input is valued and appreciated.

Suppose you—man or woman—get into such a class. How do you deal with it?

Here are some suggestions drawn from Dr. Weinrich, Tammy, Rosalie, and Christine:

- **Really listen to what is being taught.** There are some words and phrases that are red flags: denigration of men and their responsibilities, cultural relativism (anything people do is okay because it's a cultural thing), deconstructing the family, the implication that staying home with children is not a valid choice, presenting religion as oppressive or extremist.

- **Know your own beliefs.** Stand firm in what you have been taught. Stay grounded in God's Word.

- **Speak up.** It can be very hard to do, but if no one challenges what is being taught, those values will prevail. Dr. Weinrich, however, suggests that you don't speak up right away but wait and watch in the beginning. "See who in the class is open to discussion and who isn't. Don't engage those who aren't—many of them are very closed-minded. If do you try to engage them, be prepared not for a discussion but for a fight. You have to be capable of holding your own in an argument and of keeping your cool. Otherwise it will descend into a shouting match and then no learning takes place."

- **Choose your battles carefully.** "Not everything is worth challenging," says Christine. "Sometimes it's just not worth the emotional energy."

- **Talk to somebody**—friends who believe as you do, campus pastor, parents. You need to bounce what you are hearing off somebody else. Then, when you go back to class, you'll be better prepared because you will have thought and talked your responses through.

- **Be prepared to compromise.** "I don't mean on your values or religious beliefs," Christine says. "I mean when you are writing papers or giving reports, for example, just avoid talking about the things you can't compromise on. Write about the things that aren't of *eternal value*."

- **Switch classes if you can**—professors can be very different. Tammy transferred to another sociology class and found an entirely different atmosphere, one where people listened politely and all viewpoints were respected.

- **Talk to the professor in private** if you feel silenced or attacked for your beliefs. Tammy had that same sociology professor later for another class. She explained very honestly why she had transferred courses the first time. The professor, she says, moderated her personal attacks in the second course. Sometimes they don't realize what they're doing.

- **Use the class as a learning experience.** "In the long

run those classes were positive in my life because I learned about other viewpoints," says Rosalie. Christine adds, "The experience prepared me to deal with people who think that way because now I understand better where they're coming from."

Pro-Choice as the Only Acceptable View

Largely because of the feminist influence, at some colleges the view which opposes abortion is never presented or, if it is discussed, is considered unacceptable.

Christine found that to be true on her campus. "The viewpoint wasn't just pro-choice, it was pro-abortion," she says. "The validation of abortion as a good way to solve a problem and take charge of your life was very strong. It wasn't presented as 'you have a choice,' it was presented as 'this is the only way.'"

There was no pro-life group on her campus. In some other colleges pro-life groups have had trouble getting official recognition. One, at an east coast college, was denied office space in the new Women's Center (which was advertised as a place for women of diverse views to come together) until they went to court and won the right.

Here is an area where Christian students can make a difference. There are pro-life groups on most campuses. They may be small, and they may get little publicity for their activities, but they are there.

You can also speak up when abortion is presented as the only option. You may take some flack for being an "extremist," but you can point out that not all people who have moral reservations about abortion are fanatics who bomb clinics. You can testify to the fact that there are many nonextremist people who believe deeply in the sanctity of human life.

Being "Politically Correct"

Politically correct is defined by Webster as "conforming to a belief that language and practices which could offend political sensibilities (as in matters of sex or race) should be eliminated." Defined this way, political correctness is a good thing. It has raised students' awareness of how thoughtless remarks that put down a different racial or social group can inflict a great deal of pain.

As Christians we know that God created all people equal and that His love doesn't exclude anyone. Racial jokes or put-downs, sexist remarks, or humiliating mocking of a disability have no place coming from a Christian. True "political correctness" embraces the Christian view that we are all brothers and sisters in Christ and should treat each other as we would want to be treated—namely, with respect. Some groups, however, take political correctness to the extreme, allowing for only one acceptable viewpoint on "political" issues such as race, sexual preference, or abortion.

One such "extreme" was the college "speech codes" that tried to make racial or sexual remarks illegal and punishable. Most of those codes have been struck down by the courts as an infringement on the right of free speech. And there will always be some people who are ready to pounce on any slight. I remember a young woman in one of my graduate courses who seriously argued that a TV ad with a woman in a swimsuit should be banned because it contributed to the "sexual harassment culture" we live in. But such people are in the minority. Most students just want to be allowed to pursue their studies in peace and dignity.

Here again, you as a Christian student can have an influence on your campus. If you hear people denigrating others for their race or sex, speak up. You don't have to jump down their throats as the zealots do, but you can gently, in love, point out that what the speaker said has the potential to hurt someone.

And if true racial or sexual harassment takes place (and it does), you can offer support and understanding to the person being harassed and even be willing to tell what you've seen in case of disciplinary action. Your support could be a major factor in keeping someone from dropping out of school.

The grip of such radical political attitudes may be loosening on some campuses; here and there students are beginning to speak out. One young woman, a senior at an east coast university, writing in *Seventeen* magazine (September 1993), said that political correctness should be about tolerance, not shouting about whether something is insensitive or acceptable. We can only understand each other, she says, if we can freely voice and discuss our differing views.

The political world on today's campus can be intimidating, no doubt about it. But if you are prepared and go into it with the attitude that you know your own values and won't allow them to be swayed, you'll come out just fine. Not only will you succeed in your studies, but you may just have the opportunity to express some Christian values in a largely unChristian world. After all, God calls us to be the light in whatever world we find ourselves.

8

GOING HOME

Delight or Disaster?

"Going from being on my own and independent to back with my parents was like taking a step backwards," says Brad. "I felt like I'd been an adult and there I was, in the same situation I'd been in as a teenager."

That first trip home, especially if your college is far enough away that you haven't gotten back before Thanksgiving or Christmas break, can be a real eye-opener. There's a great deal of joy in renewing ties with your parents, brothers and sisters, and high school friends, but there can be a lot of stress also. Problems often surface during the longer breaks, Christmas for example, and really come to a head at the start of the first summer home. It's going to take a lot of adjustment on the part of both you and your parents to make your reintegration into their lives (and theirs into yours) go smoothly.

Since I've been a parent more recently than I've been a college student, let me first give you a glimpse into what goes on in the parental mind as a visit home or a move back home for the summer grows closer.

First, as I'm sure you won't have any trouble believing, your parents can hardly wait to see you. Even if your relationship was somewhat strained at the end of high school, all that seems to fade into the background. Your mom and dad really are looking forward to having you share your new life with them in person rather than over the phone or by e-mail. At the same time, your mom and dad are probably a bit nervous.

When a kid leaves for college, it changes the whole dynamic of the family back home. Younger brothers and sisters move into new roles: The kid who got lost in the middle is suddenly the oldest and wants to defend his new status. The baby of the family, especially if she's the only one left at home, may be reveling in her parents' undivided attention and unwilling to share it again. If you were the last to leave, your parents have undoubtedly changed their lifestyle in response to the "empty nest" and are probably enjoying the quiet house that stays so neat and the chance to eat out on the spur of the moment.

Suddenly you walk in, laundry bag slung over your shoulder (my daughter's said, "Hey, Mom, I'm Home") and everything changes.

If you've had trouble adjusting to college and have shared your homesickness or roommate fights with your parents, they may be worried and see the vacation as a chance to bolster your spirits. If your grades haven't been the greatest, they may be poised to pounce for an explanation. If you haven't yet decided on a major, they (who see endless dollars pouring out and are fearful of having to foot the bill for an extra year) may be primed with all sorts of advice and ready to exert a lot of pressure.

You, on the other hand, are probably exhausted from exams and three papers due on the same day and just want to sleep. Remember, your parents may never have experienced those pressures, or, it may have been so long ago they've forgotten how intense it can be. They may have visions of a week spent in close family time, while you have 27 friends you want to see. If you have a boy- or girlfriend you left behind, you may want to spend every available minute with him or her; Mom and Dad may not want to share you so much.

And, if you are returning for the summer, your mother may be frantically wondering where on earth to put all the things you've accumulated. I remember a friend of mine once saying, "I love having them come home, but I hate having their stuff come along!"

Add to all this your need to see yourself as an independent person—which you may assert by showing up with an ear- or nose ring—and you've set the stage for conflict.

Rikki, looking back at her college breaks from the vantage point of after-graduation independence, points out that the underlying issue is one of changing roles. "When you are away at school you're independent and you do things for yourself. When you come home, Mom and Dad feel that you're still their kid," she says. "And you are. But they may not realize how much you've been on your own. They may not respect your need to do things for yourself—even stupid things like making a dentist appointment. Your mother may make it for you. It's like, 'Mom, I can handle this. I can do this on my own.' "

"It really wasn't anything my parents did specifically," says Brad. (I'm glad he said that since he's my kid!) "It's more an issue of the situation. It's partly space—you go from having your own place, even if you share it with a roommate, to a house where you have only your bedroom and everything else is full of other people's stuff. It's partly going from thinking independently and being responsible for yourself to having Mom cook for you. It's almost an issue of pride."

In the interest of promoting better understanding and heading off problems before they start, let's look at some of the specific issues that cause conflicts between parents and returning college students and what you can do to decrease the friction.

- **A selective memory.** Realize that you may have idealized your family while you were gone. Especially if you were homesick and unsure how to fit into college society at first, you may have looked back on the past as perfect. "If only I were home with my wonderful family, I'd be so much happier" can be a seductive thought when you're lonely and out of sorts. Now you're coming home to reality: That cute little sister you missed so much still gets into your cosmetics and borrows your clothes without asking. The mother you remember as your best friend still has the same irritating habits that drove you crazy. The dad who made everything seem so safe and secure still thinks his opinion is the only valid one. Their warts may stick out much more than you remember when you are suddenly thrown together again. On the other hand, you may find yourself really appreciating your family and understanding why you missed them so much when you are together again—if that's the case, be sure to tell them.

- **Family time vs. friend time.** Mom has scheduled dinners with grandparents and aunts and uncles galore and planned a couple of shopping trips. Dad's really looking forward to time tinkering on the car or watching football like the old days. But you are barely in the door before the phone is growing out of your ear as you catch up on the lives and loves of every girl you slumber-partied with in high school, or you're lining up outings with the guys. And maybe the boy- or girlfriend you left behind is waiting on the doorstep eager for time alone. How are you going to manage all the demands?

Like most of the problems college returnees face, the answer lies in communication and compromise. Yes, you are entitled to time with your friends or the love of your life. But your parents are also entitled to some of your attention. The best thing you can do is sit down and talk about it early in the visit before resentments build up. Share with your parents what friends you want to see and what parties you want to go to. Schedule them around family obligations. Keep your priorities in order: The family should have first claim on Christmas Eve, friends can fit in on nonholiday nights. Maybe you can ease the time crunch by seeing friends in bunches, maybe Mom can schedule all the relatives at one big open house. Maybe you can spend early evenings with the family and see your friends later. Look for creative ways to fit everybody in. With planning and compromise you may be able to avoid the feeling of being stretched so thin you're likely to crack.

- **Be prepared for curfews.** Probably nothing causes more tension than the issue of "where are you going and what time will you be back?" Rikki remembers a friend down the hall who never went home for weekends or breaks, just a day or two at Christmas. Finally his friends asked why he preferred to spend all his time at college. Because, he explained, his parents made him be in by 10:00 every night he was home, no exceptions. Now, that's unreasonable. But so is demanding the right to stay out until 4:00 A.M.—your parents *are* going to worry.

Here again, a spirit of compromise can help. "In most cases if you talk to your parents when no one is mad and explain why you think they are being unreasonable, they will be receptive," says Rikki. "Calmly say, 'I feel like you guys have forgotten that I've been on my own for a while. I'm not a high school student anymore, and I think we need to change some things.'"

It's reasonable for you to want more freedom, but it's also reasonable for your parents to want to know where you are going, about what time you'll be back, and if you'll be home for dinner. It's also reasonable for them to expect a phone call if plans change or you are going to be late. You would expect that kind of behavior from any guest in your parents' home. Maybe you're not exactly a guest, but it's not asking too much for you to show some basic good manners.

- **Late nights and later mornings.** What time you leave may be just as much of an issue as what time you come in. You're used to a college schedule, which is often geared to the night owl. It's nothing after a night of studying to head out for pizza or ice cream at 10:00, 11:00, or even later. At home, 10:00 is probably pretty well bedtime. "What do you mean you're going out now? It's much too late," may be what you hear. Again, sitting down and talking it out is the only solution. You need to explain to your parents that you're used to living on a late night, later morning schedule. Point out that by going out later you'll have more time for them in the early evening. Then work out a compromise. And remember, if you do go out late and come home late, be very considerate of their sleep. You may not have to get up in the morning, but they probably do!

- **Friends.** Most parents love meeting your college friends and catching up with high school friends they may have known. Ask if you can bring your friends home—that may prevent conflicts over spending so much time away. But then be considerate—clean up after them. Remember, your mom may be used to having a neater house since you've been gone. Work out some rules with your parents: What's okay to eat and what's off limits? Is drinking by friends over 21 allowed? How late can they stay? How loud can the music be? Again, be considerate. You're on vacation but they probably have to go to work. They won't appreciate tires squealing out of the driveway at 3:00 A.M.

- **Neatness.** I know this was always an issue for me and my kids when they were home from college. I was used to having a house that, when I picked it up, stayed picked up. Shoes, books and papers, and empty glasses left sitting around drove me nuts. And I know I drove my kids nuts by telling them to clean up their rooms.

    Kristin (who is also my kid) says, "When I was at college if I got home late, I could just drop my clothes and climb into bed, if I was rushing to get ready for a date, I could leave the bathroom a disaster and deal with it later. But at home you can't do that. You're in someone else's house—yes, it's your home too, but in some ways you are almost like a guest. You have to be considerate." As her mom I would add, if you really do have to leave a mess, tell your mother why and promise to clean it up as soon as you can. Then be sure to do it.

    Living together takes compromise. You can do your part by keeping your stuff out of family areas in the house. And I'll be telling your folks in the parents' chapter to just close the door to your room and try to ignore it, remembering that it's only for a limited time.

- **Where'd you get all this stuff?** Another problem that seems to cause hysteria in many parents is the sheer volume of stuff you bring home. I remember my father grumbling about how much stuff I had in college—and I only had my clothes, a couple of lamps, and a typewriter. My kids had sofas, microwaves, filing cabinets, and bicycles! I have to confess that I *hated* having all that stuff come home. We didn't have a very big basement and I always found storing it all overwhelming. You can help. Understand how your parents feel—they want you home, they just wish there was somewhere else you could leave your stuff. Try to keep things as organized as possible. Clean things before you bring them home—a microwave with an inch of green mold is pretty hard for most moms to take. Pack stuff in sealed cartons that can be stacked neatly instead of throwing loose things in the car. And don't take it personally if your parents get a bit uptight!

- **Household changes.** You probably want to find everything at home exactly as you left it, especially your room. Well, you've changed during the time you've been away at college, isn't it reasonable to expect that your family has changed too? They have. If you've had a full-time mother during the years you were at home, you may come home to discover she's taken a job, gone back to school, or developed a whole new set of interests. Good for her—you can't be the center of her world anymore, and she can't put her life on hold so she can fill that role during the few weeks or months you are home. Your younger siblings, who may have looked up to you as their idol, have probably grown up fast and may be eager to show you how they're succeeding at your old high school. Even your room may be different—it may be part bedroom and part sewing room now. And your closet may be half full of someone else's out-of-season clothes. Some cherished childhood traditions may be changing. Maybe your mom doesn't have time to build a gingerbread house this year. Bear in mind that your family hasn't been frozen in time during the months you've been away. Try to accept the inevitable changes—they too are part of growing up.

- **Values conflicts.** You wouldn't think this would be a problem in Christian families who share the same basic values, but many times it is. Sometimes the conflicts are over religion—participating in family devotions, going to church. I've known some families in which even Christian kids decided that it should be okay for them to share a bedroom with a boy- or girlfriend over their parents' objections. Sometimes it's over drinking—the student wants to have a beer, the parents object. Sometimes it's over politics—the college returnee has adopted some liberal positions which horrify conservative parents. Sometimes it's over matters of style—an earring glinting from a guy's earlobe can set off a firestorm, so can a nose ring or a super-short miniskirt.

Some of these issues are very important, others seem trivial. But they can all produce boiling conflict and hurt feelings and can make people say things in the heat of the moment that can leave long-lasting scars.

There are a couple of important principles to remember in dealing with potential values conflicts.

First and foremost, it's still your parents' house. They are in charge and they have the right to insist that their moral principles not be violated in their home. We've talked about God's rules for our lives. If you've decided to violate those principles, you need to rethink what you're doing. Your parents have every right to say, "Not in my house." And you must respect that. That also applies to drinking if you are underage. Think about what Paul told the Romans: "Through [Jesus] and for His name's sake, we received grace and apostleship to call people from among all the Gentiles to the obedience that comes from faith. And you also are among those who are called to belong to Jesus Christ" (Romans 1:5–6). Our obedience comes from gratitude for what Christ has done for us.

The same thing goes for family devotions and going to church. I hope you have been nurturing your faith at college and will joyfully join your family at worship while you're home. If you've slipped in your church attendance while you were gone, use this opportunity to reestablish yourself with God. Maybe sharing God's Word and Sacrament with your family while you're home will inspire you to do more to strengthen your faith when you return to campus.

Matters of politics and style are a little different. Most college students need to express their individuality by setting themselves apart from their parents in some fashion. Some do it by expressing political views that differ from their parents'. The classic example was the antiwar protesters of the 1960s—families were torn apart by opposing views on Viet Nam. Many parents react to kids' new political values with the attitude "You don't know what you are talking about. Grow up." That may make the kids dig in their heels, maybe even exaggerate their new philosophy for effect. And so starts the downward spiral.

You do, of course, have the right to hold whatever political views you wish, and you also have the right to cast your vote as you see fit. But that doesn't mean you have to be obnoxious about it. If you know that you and your parents now have different political views, try to talk about them calmly, sticking to the issues with no personal attacks. If you and your parents can't do that, then don't talk about it. You can have endless political discussions back at school; why cause strife at home?

Other students express themselves through dress that parents may not approve of. Here again, why provoke a conflict? Do you really need to wear your earring at home? Do you have to bring home your most ripped-up jeans and sloppiest sweatshirt? I'm going to tell your parents in their chapter to choose their battles carefully—that matters of style and dress are rarely worth fighting over. But you can do your part by not deliberately trying to set off a crisis, tempting as it may seem.

Also be aware of advice giving and taking. Rikki has a friend whose mother asked so many questions that any conversation was like getting the third degree. "Guess what. She didn't talk to her mother very much," Rikki says. "She really closed off."

That happens all too often. Mom and Dad want to know everything about your new life but you feel your autonomy is threatened so you clam up. That makes them pry harder. It's a vicious circle, but it's one you can control. You have a right to privacy. Your parents don't have a right to pry into every area of your life and relationships at college. But understand that they do so because they care about you. They may sense that you're not happy, or you may have called home in a low moment saying how down you were and they don't realize it was just a temporary thing. They're trying to reassure themselves that you are okay and, if you aren't, to find a way to help.

Parents have a legitimate right to know what's happening with your grades and your decisions about choosing a major if they are paying for your education. You may see their concern as prying, but try to remember just how much college costs these days. They may be really sacrificing to pay the bills so they have a vested interest in how you are doing. Because not choosing a major soon enough or changing partway through can mean additional courses and more bills, they also have an interest in how you are doing in that department. Rikki remembers one friend who casually mentioned a possible interest in nursing. When she came home for the summer, her parents had lined up interviews for her at every nursing school in their state! Try not to see their questions as prying; instead, sense the financial urgency underneath. Be honest with them. If you are having trouble with grades, explain what steps you're taking (getting extra help, etc.) to improve things. Share your thinking on choosing a major. If they don't feel like they're being kept in the dark, they may not bug you so much. Panic can cause parents to clamp ever tighter in an attempt to get you "straightened out." Finally, you may need to ask them, gently and respectfully, to give you some space. If they do, reward them by being more open in the future.

Accept the fact that, for your parents, this is a bittersweet time. When you come home, especially the first time, your parents may suddenly realize how much you and their lives have changed. They may confront for the first time the realization that things will never be the same again. You will never be "home" in the same way that you were before you left for college. You will always be somewhat of a guest from now on and will never be a member of the family in quite the same way you were before. That can be tough for parents. Be sensitive to their feelings. I remember a boyfriend of my daughter's who, from the first week he went to college, referred to college as "home." His mother never said anything, but I'm sure it felt like a knife inside when he talked about going back to school as "going home." Perhaps you will come to think of college as your home—that's good, it means you've made a good adjustment. But you don't have to call it that around your parents! When you are a parent, you'll understand.

"It's a weird phase of life to be in," reflects Rikki. "I sometimes felt like I didn't belong anywhere when I was in college. You're still your parents' kid, but at the same time it's different."

It is indeed. And nowhere does the difference show up more dramatically than when you come home.

But with mutual respect, open communication, and a spirit of compromise on both sides, those vacations can be the time of warmth, renewal, and shared closeness that both you and your family are looking forward to.

9

Give This Chapter
to Your Parents

I remember the day we took our daughter, Kristin, to college. On the way, she hesitantly confessed, "It's been so long since I've had to make new friends I'm not sure I remember how." The very next day we got a phone call, "A bunch of people I didn't even know put their heads in my door last night and said, 'We're going out for ice cream, want to come?' This is going to be so much fun!"

What a change in 24 hours. Will your child adjust that quickly and find new friends that easily? Maybe. Maybe not. There are so many variables: your child's individual personality, the friendliness of that particular campus, the pure luck to be in the right place at the right time.

But one thing you can be sure of: College is a big adjustment for everyone in your family. For the student, for you as parents, for brothers and sisters. No one escapes when the basic dynamic of a family shifts, and shift it will.

To ease the transition let's take a look at some of the tasks and challenges your newly-launched offspring will face and some ways that you as parents can make the transition easier on all of you.

What's College Like Today?

If you were in college 20 or 30 years ago, you might have trouble recognizing today's campus. If you never had the chance to attend college, you may find it quite different from what you imagined. Sure, there are still the tree-shaded pathways, the ivy-covered buildings, the central square or "quad" where everyone seems to gather. But there are some new things too.

Dorms have sprouted into high-rises with floor upon floor stacked like block towers and some don't house all women or all men. There are elevators and ramps now, allowing disabled students the dorm life they may not have been able to manage in the past. The dorms are locked and room doors lock automatically (did we ever lock ours?). There's probably a security person at the front desk to make sure strangers don't wander in. No one has to sit "phone duty"—every room has a phone and probably an answering machine as well. Dorm rooms are the same ugly square boxes, but suites built around a shared bathroom are common now. And the way they are furnished has changed a great deal—while we thought ourselves adventurous to move the furniture around a bit, today's students build lofts, bring couches, TVs with VCRs, microwaves, plants, exotic lighting, and a host of other clever ideas to transform the box into home.

High tech has come to America's campuses: Computer labs, broadcast studios, elaborately-equipped sports complexes and workout centers, and videogame rooms are commonplace. Students may use computerized ID cards to both unlock their rooms and get their meals from the food service.

The student body is different too. College used to be the province of the white middle and upper class. That is no longer the case—a real gift from the God whose love embraces everyone. Students today come from a wide diversity of racial, ethnic, and socioeconomic backgrounds. There are actually more women than men in college right now, and foreign students flock to American universities. The campus is "graying" a bit as nontraditional students sit alongside 18-year-olds. Parking lots have expanded to accommodate the influx of commuter students who live at home, combining school and work.

Drugs and alcohol are so common in America's high schools that few students arrive in college without having been exposed to them; some arrive with drinking problems already in place. Today's college students probably had higher grades in high school than students of the past, but many of them need help in the basic skills—remedial programs are expanding apace. So are counseling centers, women's centers, career centers, and centers for students from every imaginable culture or lifestyle variation.

Finances are a serious problem for many of today's students—financial aid packages, jobs, and overwhelming loans are facts of life. Many students feel pressured to finish as quickly as possible and head into career fields that will allow them to meet their loan payments.

There's another major difference that makes many parents uncomfortable: Colleges used to see their roles as "in loco parentis" (Latin for "in place of a parent.") Not anymore. Colleges today, for the most part, see their students as adults who are entitled to make their own choices. In the late 1960s, the rules governing campus life largely disappeared. Some have returned, but college is not like it was for us. And that's not all bad—I'm not sure making a 22-year-old sign out and be in by 11:00 P.M. was reasonable! On the other hand, colleges have handed a lot of freedom to kids who may or may not be ready for it.

Which leads us to take a look at your student and what he or she needs to do in the next four years.

The Tasks a College Student Needs to Accomplish

According to Beverly Yahnke, Ph.D., a psychologist in private practice, most college students are moving from a rather protected environment into young adulthood. "They've been experimenting with who they are and who they will become, and they need to decide which person they've experimented with is going off to college," she laughs. "It's a time when they have the tasks of 'individuation'—becoming separate from Mom and Dad, reducing their dependency, and functioning autonomously. They are now largely in charge of determining the boundaries that are appropriate for them."

Those boundaries, she points out, may be as simple as when to come in at night or as complex as career decisions, decisions about sexuality and alcohol use, or budgeting their money to last the semester with enough left to call home for more. "They are really cast into a freefall of decisions—it's a terrible joy!" she says.

While developing his or her autonomy and independence, the college student also has to develop the skills of intimacy: making friends, living in close proximity to others, establishing relationships with the members of the opposite sex, perhaps choosing a lifemate.

While all this is going on, students also have to develop intellectually, learn new ways of thinking, new ways of putting knowledge together, new ways of using knowledge in problem-solving.

It can be quite an intimidating package.

"College can be a lot of fun for students, but it can

also include moments of abject self doubt, uncertainty, and lack of confidence in their ability to move through it to their own satisfaction and the pride of their parents," says Dr. Yahnke.

What can parents expect to happen and how can they make the transition as easy as possible for everyone? The answers to those questions are different at different stages and vary with your own needs, the needs of your individual child, and those of the siblings left behind.

The Months before the Big Move

The summer before the student heads off to college can be an especially stressful time. Kids who have been close to their families may suddenly become prickly, trying to establish some distance. "Mom, don't tell me what to do—I can do it myself," may echo through your house. Kids who have been quite independent through their younger days may also push you away, insisting "It's no big deal—I'll just throw a few things together and be gone."

"Parents can expect some *practice separations*," says Dr. Yahnke. "You may see some emotional doors closing that weren't closed before. On the other hand, you may see the doors flung wide open with a rebound into parental dependency, 'Mom, rescue me!' It can be a wildly emotional time."

Some kids, she points out, become aloof and self reliant, some don't want to even talk about it until they absolutely have to, and some want to hash over every minute detail until they drive their parents crazy. Or, they may bounce between those extremes, changing hourly.

During those last few months many parents suddenly fear they haven't really gotten all their values across to the child and are tempted to sit him or her down for a long talk about right and wrong, including lots of advice about the perils of college. That's okay, says Dr. Yahnke, but parents who have been instilling values in their children all along need to realize they are just checking to be sure the values are there, rather than giving new information. "You are underlining with a florescent marker what they already know," she says. That's not a bad thing, she points out, because it gives the departing teen a sense of reassurance, and it's a way for parents to communicate their ongoing love and concern. But be sure it's done in love, with a supportive attitude, and not by a lecture!

If parents haven't done much to communicate values to their children before, it may be too late at this point. "Those parents may panic, wondering how they can culture-proof their kids in the last three months before they leave," she says. "The answer, sadly, is 'not very effectively.' You can't teach a lifetime of values in June, July, and August." She suggests in such a circumstance that the parents and the student sit down with a third person—a minister or counselor—to talk about the crucial decisions the student will soon be making.

The Big Day Arrives

How do you say goodbye? There's nothing in the world that will ease the shock, Dr. Yahnke says. "This is a ripping and tearing away of one of the most precious people in your world. No small Band-Aid is going to do. You *are* going to notice that someone is missing in your life."

She suggests that student and parent prepare for the day rather than winging it. It's a good idea to think and talk about the kind of farewell you and your child want. Should you carry up a few boxes, hand the kid a plate of cookies and leave? Or, should you stay around, help set up the room, take your student and roommate out to dinner?

"Many kids are embarrassed by the 'windshield wiper mom' who is drenched in tears through the hugs and kisses," she says. "Other kids couldn't imagine a farewell without that." Ask your child what he or she wants, she advises, and also let your own needs be known. If you really don't want to drop off a load of stuff and be shoved out the door, say so. Find a compromise that meets everyone's needs. "Each of you should have a reasonable expectation of what is going to happen so you are insulated from any rude surprises," she says.

If you can, she suggests, take a day or two after the drop-off for a minivacation, giving yourself some time to adjust before returning to the empty house.

Once You're Back Home

You'll be inclined to call your student three times a day to see how he or she is doing. Don't. "The best course is to wait, prayerfully, for your child to call," Dr. Yahnke says. "Give the teen a chance to settle in and contact you when she's ready for an infusion of parental love and support."

Don't be surprised if you feel very real pain at first, if you cry when you pass that empty bedroom. But be aware that those feelings won't last forever. There are some advantages to the empty nest, especially if there are no other children at home: Your house stays neat and clean, there isn't nearly as much confusion, the phone doesn't ring every five minutes, you can eat out or take off for a few days on the spur of the moment. It's called mixed feelings.

You might be surprised to learn what the research says about adults' life satisfaction at various stages. While it was once thought that satisfaction would plummet once the all-absorbing job of parenting is done, the research, says Dr. Yahnke, shows just the opposite. Marital and life satisfaction is strongest right after marriage, drops with the birth of children, hits a low during their adolescence, and starts climbing again as the children leave home. Does that mean that rearing children isn't rewarding or that parents don't love their kids? Not at all. It just reflects the reality that child rearing is stressful. So don't be shocked if, as you adjust to your child being gone, you feel happy even while missing him or her. That's normal.

It can also help to choose something exciting that you've always wanted to do and plunge into it when your child leaves. For me, it was starting graduate school. Other parents have gone back to finish an interrupted college degree, started a business, accepted an intriguing job, taken on some satisfying volunteer work, plunged headlong into a craft, taken up a new sport, enlarged their work responsibilities (or shrunk them), or indulged in a hobby they never had time for before. Finding a compelling new interest can really help fill the void a departing son or daughter leaves.

"It's how you choose to navigate the next part of your family voyage that determines how pleasant the journey will be," Dr. Yahnke says.

A word to the single parent: A child's departure can leave an even bigger hole in the life of a single parent. After all, 50 percent of your family may be leaving! Many single parents feel as if their primary support system has been yanked away. The person you've shared confidences with, made plans with, shared your life with may be gone. "The grieving may be far more acute than in a family with a spouse and other children," says Dr. Yahnke. She suggests that a single parent find a support system in the church or community immediately. "You especially need to find new attachments and involvements to distract you from an unhealthy focus on the absence of your child," she says.

What about the Other Kids?

The effect one child's departing has on the other children can be radically different, depending on the family relationship prior to the child's leaving. If the family has been tightly knit, there will be a sense of loss, a feeling that part of the jigsaw puzzle is missing, reflected in the empty spot at the supper table.

On the other hand, some children are delighted when the "arch enemy" leaves. It may mean a new room or more space in a shared one. It definitely means less competition for mom-and-dad time. Many kids are so involved in their own friends and school activities, especially if they are in high school themselves, they barely notice that the older sibling is gone. "The attitude I most often see in my practice is, 'He'll be back at Christmas, now let's talk about something interesting,'" says Dr. Yahnke.

On the other hand, it can be hard on younger children, especially if the older one took special time to play with or read to them. You can help by encouraging them to communicate by videotape, audiotape, or with special phone calls of their own. Most kids won't write letters!

Use this time to get to know your remaining children in whole a new way. With the spotlight off the older one, you may find a different person in your younger one. Celebrate the new relationship and let it bloom.

The First Semester

When orientation is over, the round of parties and social activities has ended, and the academic demands have settled in, the picture changes again.

One kid may adjust smoothly and easily, be quickly absorbed into his or her new world, make friends that immediately seem joined at the hip, and find the challenges of papers and tests exhilarating.

Others may come down from the initial high with a loud thunk. Panicked phone calls: "I don't have any friends," "I can't do all this work," "I miss the dog so much" are not uncommon.

How can you help? Dr. Yahnke remembers one mother who visited her son every weekend and edited all his papers that were due the next week! "Obviously, that's not a healthy approach," she says. "You want this teen to see himself as an independent entity who seeks out Mom and Dad when needed, rather than one who feels he needs Mom and Dad to function in daily life."

Parents can ease the transition by offering a lot of love and support combining it with constant assurance that you know the student can do it and you have confidence that he or she will make good decisions. Phone calls are great, but so are letters. Parents may not realize the lift a letter in the mailbox can give—it can be read and reread whenever the student is down. E-mail can be quick and efficient and give a student a daily boost. And of course, packages from home are welcome at any time, especially if they hold treats to share with friends and dorm mates. If you're worried about something—sleeping, or eating well, or some other topic—a magazine article clipped and mailed can get the message across better than a lecture.

"It's important to communicate to your student that you are perpetually available, a phone call away," says Dr. Yahnke. "That provides an important safety net for the teen who is taking those first steps across the high wire of life."

The first visit home will bring its own strains. You may envision the reunion in glowing detail, but reality may be a little different. You may see a real change in your student, a healthy sense of independence and autonomy. That, of course, is good. It's what you hoped would happen in college. But it can also bring stress and strain as the newly-emancipated student fights every restriction. Read the chapter on coming home—see what other college students say bugged them the most about returning to the bosom of the family and perhaps adjust your expectations a bit. That doesn't mean you should take off all the reins and allow the student to live in your home as if it were a dorm. You have a right to reasonable order and to know where the student is going and when he's coming home. But use other students' suggestions to effect some compromises that will help make the reunion as happy and joy-filled as you picture it.

If Crisis Strikes

It's the phone call that chills every parent's heart: "Mom, I'm *so* homesick, I want to quit and come home," "Dad, there's been an accident," "I'm *so* sick, I think I need a doctor."

Bad things do happen to college students—paralyzing unhappiness, being the victim of a rape or other crime, broken limbs, severe mono. We all pray for our kids that such awful things will never befall them, but sometimes they happen anyway. How does a parent respond when the crisis is real?

First, the severely homesick student: That's more rare than common, says Dr. Yahnke, but it does happen. Phone contact may not be enough in this case; you may need to make a visit. The message you want to send, she says, is "We are here for you, we're available, we believe in the choices we've made together, we want to assure you that we care about what you're going through, but we believe that you and God working together will be able to succeed." She suggests that you enlist the aid of a counselor at the school who is trained and experienced in dealing with student adjustment to help you and the student work through it.

If that doesn't work and the child still insists on coming home, what then? "If your child for some reason— overwhelming anxiety or depression—can't function in the school, then making her stay there for a semester may simply convince the student that she is a loser," she says. "She can feel such shame that a downward spiral can develop very quickly." She points out that there is no hard and fast rule, and each case must be decided on its individual merit. You need to work with the school and the student and come to a joint decision in the student's best interest.

A student who is in medical peril, either through an accident or illness, probably needs a parent there if at all possible. Colleges have health services and will arrange hospitalization for a student when necessary, but it's a tough situation, especially for a freshman, to be in the hospital a long way from home and family support.

Some students have been victims of crime on campus. Robberies and other assaults are not unknown, and rapes happen more than many parents and students realize. Being a crime victim can rock a student to the core. Many drop out of college, some never come back. But others manage somehow to get past it and go on with life. Dr. Yahnke remembers a young woman who was raped. "She battled seriously with whether she should stay in school," she recalls. "Her parents came to her side and told her they hoped she would be able to continue since she'd been off to such a good start, but that they would understand if she decided to take some time off. Just having their support and understanding helped her to decide to continue." You can't decide for your child in a tragic circumstance, all you can do is provide as much emotional support as possible and let the student make the decision. This is certainly an instance where professional counseling is called for.

Another circumstance that can be tough to deal with is when your student has a friend or roommate who is in serious trouble from drinking, using drugs, or sleeping around, or is depressed and suicidal. Your child can become the caretaker for the friend and it can have a serious impact on his or her happiness and schoolwork. Parents need to listen, to offer advice, to encourage their student to push the friend into getting professional help. If nothing is working and you feel your child's education is at risk, you may have to become his or her advocate. "In many circumstances it's good to let your student solve the problem, but sometimes parents have to go to bat for their child because the kid doesn't have the savvy or the clout to get it fixed alone," Dr. Yahnke says. "The situation needs to be brought to the attention of the RA or the administration. A student with deep problems needs special care; you may have to push to be sure he or she gets it."

Sending a child off to college is a special time for all parents: a time of joy, of sadness, of stress, of relief. And it's also a time for a lot of prayer.

Dr. Yahnke reminds us, "No one can launch a son or daughter without placing that child into God's care and keeping. When you are trusting Christian parents who recognize that we have a God of grace and love, you have the capacity to trust that in Mom and Dad's absence they have a heavenly Father who will continue to care for them, meet their needs, and provide them with every possible blessing—and that makes it a little easier to let go."

Leaving time is also a time to celebrate what you've done right, she says. "Celebrate your love and commitment to God, to one another, and to your children," she says. "You've done your best to create a home where spiritual values have guided your lives, you've done your best to support your children as they discover who they are and who God yet wants them to be, you've helped them learn compassion, responsibility, and the love of their Savior. Trust that they are safe in that love."

FOOD GUIDE PYRAMID
A GUIDE TO DAILY FOOD CHOICES

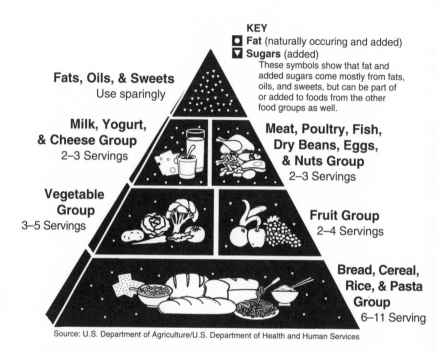

KEY
■ **Fat** (naturally occuring and added)
▼ **Sugars** (added)
These symbols show that fat and added sugars come mostly from fats, oils, and sweets, but can be part of or added to foods from the other food groups as well.

Fats, Oils, & Sweets
Use sparingly

Milk, Yogurt, & Cheese Group
2–3 Servings

Meat, Poultry, Fish, Dry Beans, Eggs, & Nuts Group
2–3 Servings

Vegetable Group
3–5 Servings

Fruit Group
2–4 Servings

Bread, Cereal, Rice, & Pasta Group
6–11 Serving

Source: U.S. Department of Agriculture/U.S. Department of Health and Human Services